Once Upon A Time

Fairy Tales in the Library and Language Arts Classroom for Grades 3-6

Jane Heitman

Linworth Books

Professional Development Resources for
K-12 Library Media and Technology Specialists

Library of Congress Cataloging-in-Publication Data

Heitman, Jane.
  Once upon a time : fairy tales in the library and language arts classroom for grades 3-6 / Jane Heitman.
    p. cm.
  Includes bibliographical references and index.
  ISBN 1-58683-231-X (pbk.)
 1. Language arts (Elementary)--United States. 2. Reading (Elementary)--United States. 3. Fairy tales. I. Title.
  LB1576.H3325 2007
  372.64--dc22
                                  2007006890

Cynthia Anderson: Acquisitions Editor
Carol Simpson: Editorial Director
Judi Repman: Consulting Editor

Published by Linworth Publishing, Inc.
3650 Olentangy River Road, Suite 250
Columbus, Ohio 43214

Copyright © 2007 by Linworth Publishing, Inc.

All rights reserved. Purchasing this book entitles a librarian to reproduce activity sheets for use in the library within a school or entitles a teacher to reproduce activity sheets for single classroom use within a school. Other portions of the book (up to 15 pages) may be copied for staff development purposes within a single school. Standard citation information should appear on each page. The reproduction of any part of this book for an entire school or school system or for commercial use is strictly prohibited. No part of this book may be electronically reproduced, transmitted or recorded without written permission from the publisher.

ISBN: 1-58683-231-X

Table of Contents

About the Author v
Acknowledgments v
Table of Figures vi
Table of Skills Applied to Lessons vii
Standards for the English Language Arts Sponsored by NCTE and IRA x
Information Literacy Standards for Student Learning xi
Introduction xii
   Why Use Fairy Tales? xii
   Collaboration xiii
How to Use This Book xv

SECTION I: The Fairy Tales 1
   What is a Fairy Tale? 1
   Cinderella 2
      Sources Consulted 3
      Selected Annotated Bibliography 3
   Rapunzel 10
      Sources Consulted 11
      Selected Annotated Bibliography 11
   Sleeping Beauty 14
      Sources Consulted 14
      Selected Annotated Bibliography 14
   Beauty and the Beast 16
      Sources Consulted 17
      Selected Annotated Bibliography 17
   Snow White 19
      Sources Consulted 19
      Selected Annotated Bibliography 20
   Rumpelstiltskin 21
      Sources Consulted 21
      Selected Annotated Bibliography 22
   Jack and the Beanstalk 23
      Sources Consulted 24
      Selected Annotated Bibliography 24
   Hansel and Gretel 28
      Sources Consulted 28
      Selected Annotated Bibliography 29

SECTION II: The Lessons 31
   Reading 31
      Fairy Tale Dictionary 31
         Alternate Activity 32
      Repeat After Me 32
      Commonalities 32
         Extended Activity 34

Table of Contents continued

Story Element Study 34
    Plot 34
        Map That Plot 34
        Putting It Together 37
            Alternate Activity 37
        Four Main Things Sandwich 37
            Extended Activity 38
        Confounded Conflict 38
    Types of Conflict 41
        Plot Ping-Pong 41
        Once Upon a Beginning 41
        Resolved! 44
        And Then What Happened? 44
            Alternate Activity 44
        What If? 46
            Extended Activity 46
        Making Connections 47
            Extended Activity 47
    Character 49
        Type Them 49
            Extended Activity 49
        Fairy Tale Coat of Arms 51
        Troublesome and Trouble Free Traits 51
        How Does the Character Feel? 54
    Setting 54
        Time and Again 54
        Replaced Fairy Tales 57
            Extended Activity 57
    Theme 57
        The Big Picture 57
        It's a Classic 58
            Extended Activity 58
Assessment Suggestions 61
    Fairy Tale Bingo 61
        Alternate Activity 63
    Self Assessment 63
    Peer Assessment 63
    Library Media Specialist and Teacher Assessment 63
    Assessment Resources 65
Writing 66
    Compare and Contrast 66
        Tales Alike 66
            Resources About Writing Essays 66
            Alternate Activity 66
        Hooray for Differences 68
            Alternate Activity 68

Table of Contents continued

Writing Story Elements 68
   Plot 68
      What Could Happen Next? 68
      Tag Team Tales 69
         Alternate Activity 69
      Beyond Once Upon a Time 73
         Extended Activity 73
      New Beginnings 74
      Conflict Makes the Tale 76
      Obstacle Course 76
      Good Endings 79
      You Said It 82
      Fairy Tale Tribune 82
         Extended Activity 83
      You're Invited 83
      Write Original Fairy Tale 83
      Fractured Fairy Tale 85
         Alternate Activity 85
      Script It 85
      From Fairy Tale to Fact 86
      Poetic Fairy Tales 86
      Cook It Up! 88
   Character 88
      Character Acrostic 88
      Wanted—Enchanted or Not 90
         Extended Activity 90
      Character Profile 90
      Who Am I? 93
      Fairy Tale Character Résumé 93
      It's My Business 95
         Alternate Activity 95
      Add a Character 97
         Alternate Activity 97
   Setting 98
      Fairy Tale Now 98
         Alternate Activity 98
      For Sale 98
      Move It 100
   Theme 100
      My Life Is Like a Fairy Tale 100
      Flip the Theme 101
Assessment Suggestions 101
   Self Assessment 101
   Peer Assessment 101
   Library Media Specialist and Teacher Assessment 101

Table of Contents continued

SECTION III: Speaking and Listening 103
   Read Aloud 103
      Read Aloud to a Pet 104
      Read Aloud Audio Recordings 104
      Read Aloud to a Partner 105
      Read Aloud to a Class 105
         Extended Activity 105
     Assessment Suggestions for Reading Aloud 106
   Storytelling 107
      Storytelling Practice 107
      Ready, Set, Tell 109
      Storytelling Festival 109
     Assessment Suggestions for Storytelling 109
   Choral Reading 110
      Read It Together 110
     Assessment Suggestions for Choral Reading 111
   Readers Theater 111
      Reading as Play 111
     Assessment Suggestions for Readers Theater 113
   Puppet Theater 113
      Puppet Theater Resources 113
      Puppet Play 114
   Drama 115
      The Play's the Thing 115
         Alternate Activity 115
         Script Sources 115
     Assessment Suggestions for Drama 115
      Fairy Tale Talk Show 116
      Guilty or Not Guilty? 120
         Alternate Activity 121
         Extended Activity 121
   Listening 122
     Assessment Suggestions for Listening 122

Works Cited 124

Index 128

About the Author

Jane Heitman, former school teacher and librarian, has worked in education for 25 years. She wrote Linworth's *Teach Writing to Older Readers Using Picture Books: Every Picture Tells a Story* (2004) and *Rhymes and Reasons: Librarians and Teachers Using Poetry to Foster Literacy* (2003). She speaks to librarians, teachers, and literacy coaches about these topics, and was selected to appear in a future volume of Thomson Gale's *Something About the Author*.

Jane has published poetry, curriculum, activities, and other material for children and teachers in church settings. Originally from South Dakota, she now lives in Grand Junction, Colorado. She manages the interlibrary loan unit at Mesa State College and volunteers in the children's center at the public library there.

Acknowledgments

Many thanks to all who assisted and encouraged me through this process, especially my project manager, Sherry York, the enthusiastic staff of the Mesa County Public Library Children's Center, Mesa State College Library staff, Sue Karlen, Karen Schniederjan, Riana Kettle, Becky Meyer, Linda Armstrong, the faithful members of my writers groups, and my school librarian and teacher friends.

Table of Figures

Figure A	**TABLE OF SKILLS APPLIED TO LESSONS**	vii
Figure 1.1	*Commonalities Template*	33
Figure 1.2	*Story Map Example*	35
Figure 1.3	*Story Map Template*	36
Figure 1.4	*Four Main Things Sandwich*	39
Figure 1.5	*Confounded Conflict Worksheet*	40
Figure 1.6	*Plot Ping-Pong*	42
Figure 1.7	*Once Upon a Beginning*	43
Figure 1.8	*Resolved! Worksheet*	45
Figure 1.9	*Making Connections Worksheet*	48
Figure 1.10	*Type Them*	50
Figure 1.11	*Fairy Tale Coat of Arms Template*	52
Figure 1.12	*Trouble and Traits*	53
Figure 1.13	*How Does the Character Feel?*	55
Figure 1.14	*Time and Again Worksheet*	56
Figure 1.15	*Replaced Fairy Tales*	59
Figure 1.16	*The Big Picture Worksheet*	60
Figure 1.17	*Fairy Tale Bingo Template*	62
Figure 1.18	*Cinderella Bingo Sample*	61
Figure 1.19	*Peer Assessment Template*	64
Figure 1.20	*Sample Rubric: Reading Inference*	65
Figure 2.1	*Tales Alike*	67
Figure 2.2	*Hooray for Differences*	70
Figure 2.3	*What Could Happen Next? Evaluation*	71
Figure 2.4	*Beyond Once Upon a Time Assessment*	72
Figure 2.5	*New Beginnings*	75
Figure 2.6	*Conflict Makes the Tale*	77
Figure 2.7	*Obstacle Course*	78
Figure 2.8	*Good Endings*	80
Figure 2.9	*Good Endings Assessment*	81
Figure 2.10	*You're Invited Template*	84
Figure 2.11	*From Fairy Tale to Fact Planning Sheet*	87
Figure 2.12	*Cook It Up! Template*	89
Figure 2.13	*Wanted—Enchanted or Not*	91
Figure 2.14	*Character Profile Planning Sheet*	92
Figure 2.15	*Fairy Tale Resumé*	94
Figure 2.16	*It's My Business Template*	96
Figure 2.17	*For Sale*	99
Figure 2.18	*Sample Rubric: Writing Sequencing*	102
Figure 3.1	*Sample Rubric for Speaking Activities*	106
Figure 3.2	*Storytelling Critique Sheet*	108
Figure 3.3	*Character Qualities Planning Template*	117
Figure 3.4	*Emcee Planning Template*	118
Figure 3.5	*Talk Show Assessment Template*	119
Figure 3.6	*Listening Peer Assessment Template*	123

Table of Skills Applied to Lessons

In the table below, each lesson is listed and correlated with the skills it teaches. Refer to the Table of Contents for lesson page.

Lesson	Cause & Effect	Compre-hension	Context	Critical Thinking	Fluency	Inference	Main Action	Pattern Recognition	Predicting Skills	Research	Sequencing	Story Structure
Fairy Tale Dictionary		●	●									
Repeat After Me								●	●			●
Commonalities & Figure 1.1								●				
Map That Plot & Figure 1.3		●										●
Putting It Together				●							●	
Four Main Things Sandwich & Figure 1.4		●					●					
Confounded Conflict & Figure 1.5	●	●		●								
Plot Ping-Pong & Figure 1.6	●	●		●								
Once Upon a Beginning & Figure 1.7		●		●								●
Resolved! & Figure 1.8		●		●								●
And Then What Happened?				●		●			●			
What If?		●				●			●			
Making Connections & Figure 1.9		●		●				●				
Type Them & Figure 1.10		●	●					●				
Fairy Tale Coat of Arms & Figure 1.11		●		●		●			●			
Troublesome and Trouble Free Traits & Figure 1.12		●		●		●			●			
How Does the Character Feel? & Figure 1.13		●				●			●			
Time and Again & Figure 1.14		●	●			●			●			
Replaced Fairy Tales & Figure 1.15				●		●			●			
The Big Picture & Figure 1.16		●		●								
It's a Classic		●		●						●		
Tales Alike & Figure 2.1				●				●				
Hooray for Differences & Figure 2.2				●				●				
What Could Happen Next? & Figure 2.3				●					●			
Tag Team				●							●	

Figure A: Table of Skills Applied to Lessons

Table of Skills Applied to Lessons continued

Lesson	Cause & Effect	Compre-hensio	Context	Critical Thinking	Fluency	Inference	Main Action	Pattern Recognition	Predicting Skills	Research	Sequencing	Story Structure
Tales												
Beyond Once Upon a Time & Figure 2.4		●		●								
New Beginnings & Figure 2.5				●								●
Conflict Makes the Tale & Figure 2.6		●							●			
Obstacle Course & Figure 2.7		●					●					●
Good Endings & Figures 2.8 & 2.9				●					●			●
You Said It				●			●					
Fairy Tale Tribune		●		●								●
You're Invited & Figure 2.10		●				●						
Write Original Fairy Tale		●							●			●
Fractured Fairy Tale		●		●								●
Script It		●		●								●
From Fairy Tale to Fact & Figure 2.11		●		●						●		
Poetic Fairy Tales		●		●								
Cook It Up! & Figure 2.12				●		●				●		
Character Acrostic		●		●								
Wanted—Enchanted or Not & Figure 2.13		●				●						
Character Profile & Figure 2.14		●				●						
Who Am I?		●										
Fairy Tale Character Resumé & Figure 2.15				●		●						
It's My Business & Figure 2.16		●		●		●						
Add a Character						●						●
Fairy Tale Now		●	●									
For Sale				●		●						
Move It		●				●						
My Life Is Like a Fairy Tale		●				●						
Flip the Theme		●				●						
Read Aloud to a Pet					●							

viii *Once Upon A Time: Fairy Tales in the Library and Language Arts Classroom, Grades 3-6*

Table of Skills Applied to Lessons continued

Lesson	Cause & Effect	Compre-hensio	Context	Critical Thinking	Fluency	Inference	Main Action	Pattern Recognition	Predicting Skills	Research	Sequencing	Story Structure
Read Aloud Audio Recordings					●							
Read Aloud to a Partner		●			●							
Read Aloud to a Class		●			●							
Storytelling Practice Figure 3.1		●		●	●							
Ready, Set, Tell		●		●	●							
Storytelling Festival		●		●	●							
Read It Together		●		●	●							
Reading as Play		●		●	●							
Puppet Play		●		●	●							
The Play's the Thing		●		●	●							
Fairy Tale Talk Show & Figures 3.2, 3.3		●		●	●	●						
Guilty or Not Guilty	●	●		●		●	●					

Table of Skills Applied to Lessons ix

Standards for the English Language Arts

Sponsored by NCTE and IRA

The vision guiding these standards is that all students must have the opportunities and resources to develop the language skills they need to pursue life's goals and to participate fully as informed, productive members of society. These standards assume that literacy growth begins before children enter school as they experience and experiment with literacy activities—reading and writing, and associating spoken words with their graphic representations. Recognizing this fact, these standards encourage the development of curriculum and instruction that make productive use of the emerging literacy abilities that children bring to school. Furthermore, the standards provide ample room for the innovation and creativity essential to teaching and learning. They are not prescriptions for particular curriculum or instruction. Although we present these standards as a list, we want to emphasize that they are not distinct and separable; they are, in fact, interrelated and should be considered as a whole.

1. Students read a wide range of print and non-print texts to build an understanding of texts, of themselves, and of the cultures of the United States and the world; to acquire new information; to respond to the needs and demands of society and the workplace; and for personal fulfillment. Among these texts are fiction and nonfiction, classic and contemporary works.

2. Students read a wide range of literature from many periods in many genres to build an understanding of the many dimensions (e.g., philosophical, ethical, aesthetic) of human experience.

3. Students apply a wide range of strategies to comprehend, interpret, evaluate, and appreciate texts. They draw on their prior experience, their interactions with other readers and writers, their knowledge of word meaning and of other texts, their word identification strategies, and their understanding of textual features (e.g., sound-letter correspondence, sentence structure, context, graphics).

4. Students adjust their use of spoken, written, and visual language (e.g., conventions, style, vocabulary) to communicate effectively with a variety of audiences and for different purposes.
5. Students employ a wide range of strategies as they write and use different writing process elements appropriately to communicate with different audiences for a variety of purposes.
6. Students apply knowledge of language structure, language conventions (e.g., spelling and punctuation), media techniques, figurative language, and genre to create, critique, and discuss print and non-print texts.
7. Students conduct research on issues and interests by generating ideas and questions, and by posing problems. They gather, evaluate, and synthesize data from a variety of sources (e.g., print and non-print texts, artifacts, people) to communicate their discoveries in ways that suit their purpose and audience.
8. Students use a variety of technological and information resources (e.g., libraries, databases, computer networks, video) to gather and synthesize information and to create and communicate knowledge.
9. Students develop an understanding of and respect for diversity in language use, patterns, and dialects across cultures, ethnic groups, geographic regions, and social roles.
10. Students whose first language is not English make use of their first language to develop competency in the English language arts and to develop understanding of content across the curriculum.
11. Students participate as knowledgeable, reflective, creative, and critical members of a variety of literacy communities.
12. Students use spoken, written, and visual language to accomplish their own purposes (e.g., for learning, enjoyment, persuasion, and the exchange of information).

Standards for the English Language Arts, by the International Reading Association and the National Council of Teachers of English, Copyright 1996 by the International Reading Association and the National Council of Teachers of English. Reprinted with permission.

Information Literacy Standards for Student Learning

Information Literacy Standards by the American Association of School Librarians (AASL) can be found at the American Library Association Web site at <www.ala.org/ala/aasl/aaslproftools/informationpower/InformationLiteracyStandards_final.pdf>.

Introduction

Once upon a time, a librarian observed students enjoying fairy tales and their many adaptations. The librarian also heard students grumble and mumble about their language arts work. Then she heard language arts teachers grumble and mumble about how to help students gain proficiency and meet standards. The librarian knew that no fairy godmother or magic beans would solve this problem, but fairy tales might.

The librarian gathered some beloved fairy tales and some ideas. She took them to a language arts teacher. Together, they walked through the forest of lesson planning and teaching, mindful of lurking dangers. They started with something students already knew—fairy tales—and applied reading, writing, and speaking components to the tales. Students were so enchanted by the stories that they stopped thinking of the work as evil. They no longer sat staring at their papers, waiting for a supernatural helper to complete their work. Best of all, when students mastered a lesson, they felt like kings and queens.

Whether this tale ends happily ever after depends on several variables. This book, while not magic, is a guide for well-planned, American Association of School Librarians (AASL) and National Council of Teachers of English (NCTE) standards-based language arts lessons using fairy tales for grades three through six.

Why Use Fairy Tales?

Fairy tales began in folklore, often centuries, or even millennia, ago. They have become part of the culture, and part of the canon of children's literature. Even if students have never heard the original tales, they have seen movies or heard allusions to tales. Teaching based on fairy tales offers familiarity to students and gives them a foundation upon which to build.

Fairy tales are widely available. Your library already has fairy tale anthologies and separate titles in a variety of versions, and others are easy to find. Many tales are free online.

Fairy tales are cross-cultural. You and your students will be amazed at how these tales have traveled and been interpreted and retold in a variety of cultures. They can help students understand other cultures and resonate with their own.

Jack Zipes explains that though fairy tales were not originally intended for children, they have been written with children in mind at least since Charles Perrault wrote his collections in the 1600's, Madame d'Aulnoy and Madame Le Prince de Beaumont wrote theirs in the 1700's, and the Grimm brothers wrote theirs in the 1800's. Tales moved from the French salons to the nursery, and from the German folk to their kinder (*When* 12, 15-16, 18).

Fairy tales hold appeal for children for many reasons, depending on which expert you read. "When introduced to fairy tales, children welcome them mainly because the stories nurture their great desire for change and independence" (Zipes, *When* 1). "Fairy tales, unlike any other form of literature, direct the child to discover his identity and calling, and they also suggest what experiences are needed to develop his character further" (Bettelheim 24). "Yet the hold these stories have on the imagination of children is so compelling that it becomes difficult to conceive of a childhood without them. Growing up without fairy tales implies spiritual impoverishment, as one writer after another has warned" (Tatar xiv).

Though many scholars have studied historical, political, social, psychological, linguistic, and literary aspects of fairy tales, the purpose here is to enjoy the stories and use them as a basis for language arts applications.

Collaboration

"How can we best help our students gain proficiency in language arts?" This question should be foremost in goal setting and lesson-planning. Collaboration among willing partners with proficiency as the goal creates a team atmosphere. When two or more school staff collaborate, staff feel less alone in achieving goals. Lessons are reinforced and may be approached in different ways so that a variety of learning styles are addressed and various points of view are offered.

In general, librarians are the research and resources experts, while classroom teachers are the subject experts. The amount of collaboration that takes place depends on the partners' personalities, school schedules, the lessons themselves, and other factors. The partners should decide the following, based on each lesson:

- What are the lesson's objectives?
- Which standards will be addressed?
- Who will lead the lesson, or who will lead which parts of the lesson?
- Where will the lesson take place—in the library, in the classroom, or parts in both?
- What resources and materials are needed and who will prepare them?
- How will the lesson's effectiveness be assessed?

For more information about collaboration, see

American Association of School Librarians, and Association for Educational Communications and Technology. *Information Power: Building Partnerships for Learning*. Chicago: American Library Assn., 1998.

Buzzeo, Toni. *Collaborating to Meet Standards: Teacher/Librarian Partnerships for K-6*. Worthington, OH: Linworth, 2002.

Glandon, Shan. *Integrating Technology: Effective Tools for Collaboration*. Worthington, OH: Linworth, 2002.

Once Upon a Time will help librarians and teachers kill the ogres of boredom and set students on a path toward proficiency, steeped in well-known folklore.

How to Use This Book

The first section of *Once Upon a Time* contains background information about fairy tales in general and eight specific fairy tale titles. An annotated, selected list of adaptations appropriate for grades three through six accompanies each tale. Anthologies, Disney, and multimedia versions have not been included. The selected books are in print at the time of this writing. Librarians and teachers may use this section for their own reference and to guide students to tales similar to those they have already read. Educators can apply information from this section to language arts, social sciences, multicultural lessons, and English language learners.

The book's second section contains lessons for reading, writing, speaking, and listening. Assessment suggestions, sample rubrics, recommendations, and resources accompany each section. Each lesson:

- Lists the specific AASL and NCTE standards that apply
- Can be used with the fairy tales mentioned in the first section or any tales the leaders or students choose
- Can be led by librarians, by teachers, or by librarians and teachers collaborating together
- May be held in the library, the classroom, or other venues
- Requires minimal preparation and inexpensive supplies and equipment though some lessons will take more than one class period

Reproducible templates, worksheets, planning guides, and sample rubrics are included where appropriate, as listed in the Table of Figures and the Table of Skills Applied to Lessons. Though intended to support specific lessons, many of the reproducibles may be adapted to your own lessons. These reproducibles aid in planning and guide students' thinking.

Educators must take care to stay within copyright law and guidelines, helping students apply AASL Information Literacy Standard 8, using ethical behavior when using information and information technology. Proper, legal use of published material depends on several factors depending on circumstances. For guidance, see your school's policies and the following sources:

Simpson, Carol. *Copyright Catechism: Practical Answers to Real Copyright Questions from Educators.* Worthington, OH: Linworth, 2005.

—-. *Copyright for Schools: A Practical Guide.* 4th ed. Worthington, OH: Linworth, 2005.

—-. *Copyright Responsibilities for Educators...Quick Pocket Guide.* Worthington, OH: Linworth, [2005].

The list of works cited will guide librarians and teachers to other valuable resources, and the index will help readers quickly find what they need within the book.

Section I

The Fairy Tales

What is a Fairy Tale?

Though people may instinctively know what is meant by "fairy tale," a true definition is more difficult. Folklore and fairy tales are closely related, but fairy tales can be considered a subgenre of folklore. Other subgenres of folklore are myths and legends, according to Heidi Anne Heiner's "What Is a Fairy Tale?" Fairy tales originated as folk tales passed down orally from generation to generation and from place to place. Waller Hastings, in his online article "Defining the Fairy Tale" says that the term "fairy tales" applied when the tales were written down and given a more fixed form.

The term "fairy tale" comes from Madame d'Aulnoy's *Contes des fées*, published in France in 1698 and translated into English in 1699 as *Tales of the Fairys*. The Oxford English Dictionary traces the term back to 1749 (Opie 17-18). The stories have been called "fairy tales" ever since, although many fairy tales do not contain fairies at all.

Fairy tales have these traits in common:

- They are unbelievable
- They contain supernatural elements
- They contain stereotyped characters
- They have undefined time and place as setting (Opie 18-19)

Many fairy tales and some of their retellings contain gruesome violence and fearful situations. The books selected for inclusion in the annotated bibliographies for each tale were chosen for their appropriateness for third through sixth grades. However, they are not necessarily violence or fear free. A librarian's or teacher's presentation and discussion of material can help prevent students' nightmares. Educators should preview materials their students will be using, considering their own sensibilities, the students' ages and personalities, the school's philosophy, and community standards.

An amazing amount of scholarship by folklorists traces the commonalities and origins of folk and fairy tales. The standard work in this realm is Antti Aarne's *The Types of the Folktale, a Classification and Bibliography*. Since Aarne's first international classification index in 1910 and its refinement by Stith Thompson in 1928, scholars have referred to tales by AT number, the number of the type of tale. Such a system helps us see the connections among tales, the movement of a tale from region to region, and a general view of a specific tale. AT numbers and labels are included in the brief histories of the selected tales that follow to enable readers to examine modern, original tales in the larger folklore context and draw their own connections.

The eight tales included here with histories and discussions were chosen because they

- Are well known
- Have many adaptations
- Include a variety of cultures
- Have themes that students can understand
- Have humans as main characters

From oral tellings in ancient times to written tales in European courts to written and multimedia versions for children and their families, fairy tales continue to delight and inform us.

Cinderella

"Cinderella," "Rashin Coatie," "Aschenputtel," "Finetta," "Zezolla"—no matter what you call her, she's the main character of one of the oldest, best known, and most loved fairy tales. Experts believe that before anyone wrote down a version of "Cinderella," people knew the story and told it from generation to generation. The first written account, "Yeh-shen," is credited to Tuan Ch'eng in China in approximately 850 A.D. Today somewhere between 350 and 1500 versions exist, depending on which media and variant types are counted. New versions continue to be written and produced in books, plays, TV shows, and movies.

Most English-speakers identify Charles Perrault as author of "Cinderella." The Perrault version was published in 1697 in Paris. Written for Paris's salon society, Perrault made the tale more fanciful and less violent than some other versions. Perrault originated the pumpkin coach, the rodent coachmen, and the glass slipper so familiar to our modern culture. The happily-ever-after, all-is-forgiven ending seemed just right for his polite society audience.

The German Grimm brothers' version, "Aschenputtel," published in 1812, is another well-known version in English. This earthier version includes a tree and birds rather than a fairy godmother. It also contains more violence, with the stepsisters cutting off parts of their feet to fit the shoe. While Aschenputtel lives happily-ever-after, this

> **Themes**
> - Virtue
> - Beauty
> - Kindness
> - Jealousy
> - Sibling rivalry
> - What other themes can you and your students find?

version offers retribution on the evil stepsisters, with birds pecking their eyes out.

Literature and social sciences scholars have examined, analyzed, and classified the story for centuries. The AT Index classifies "Cinderella" as the "Persecuted Heroine" type of tale. In 1892, Marian Roalfe Cox published *Cinderella: Three Hundred and Forty-Five Variants of Cinderella, Catskin, and Cap O' Rushes, abstracted and tabulated*. Still a valuable resource, it is available online at Heidi Anne Heiner's *SurLaLune Fairy Tales* Web site (www.surlalunefairytales.com).

Different cultures tell the tale differently, and in some versions, the main character is male. Certain characteristics hold true in all versions, however. In each story, family, sometimes emphasizing sibling rivalry, abuses the downtrodden main character. A fairy godmother or other creature (a fish, birds, or a calf, for example) rescues the main character. The main character must not reveal his or her true identity. Royalty identifies the main character by the character's left-behind object, often a shoe. The main character in every version lives happily ever after, but his or her wicked family does not always share that luck. Some versions have violent ends for those who have harmed the main character.

Sources Consulted

Aarne, Antti. *The Types of the Folktale, a Classification and Bibliography*. Helsinki, Finland: Suomalainen Tiedeakatemia, 1961.

Bettelheim, Bruno. *Uses of Enchantment*. New York: Knopf, 1977.

Heiner, Heidi Anne. "History of Cinderella." *SurLaLune Fairy Tales*. 1 Dec. 2004. 02 June 2007<www.surlalunefairytales.com/cinderella/history.html>.

Hollenbeck, Kathleen M. *Teaching with Cinderella Stories from Around the World*. New York: Scholastic, 2003.

Kready, Laura F. *A Study of Fairy Tales*. Boston: Houghton, 1916.

Opie, Iona and Peter Opie. *The Classic Fairy Tales*. New York: Oxford UP, 1974.

Selected Annotated Bibliography

Climo, Shirley. *The Egyptian Cinderella*. Illus. Ruth Heller. New York: HarperCollins, 1989. 32 p. Set in the sixth century B.C., Rhodopis, a Greek girl, is sold into slavery in Egypt. The Egyptian girls tease her because she looks different, so Rhodopis befriends animals and dances with them. Her master sees her and promises her fancy slippers. The other girls are jealous. The household is invited to the Pharaoh's in Memphis, but Rhodopis has to stay home. A falcon, the symbol of the Egyptian god Horus, comes to Rhodopis and takes one of her slippers. He drops the slipper in the Pharaoh's lap. Pharaoh sees this as a gift from God and leaves to search for the slipper's owner. The Egyptian girls arrive at Pharaoh's to find a deserted throne and streets, so they go back home. Pharaoh's barge comes to Rhodopis's house. She hides but is drawn out. The slipper fits, she joins Pharaoh on his barge, and they live happily ever after. An author note gives historical information. Fine Egyptian-style art helps readers imagine the scenes.

—. *The Irish Cinderlad*. Illus. Loretta Krupinski. New York: Harper, 1996. 32 p. Here is a version with a boy, Becan (meaning "small") as the main character. Becan becomes a herd boy and befriends a mad bull that turns out to be magic. The bull talks to Becan and provides food for him. Becan's stepmother and stepsisters find out and prepare to butcher the bull. Becan rides him away, where the bull must fight a gray bull and die. The bull asks Becan to twist off his tail after it's dead. Becan wears the bull's tail as a belt and uses it to conquer a giant. He saves Princess Finola from being sacrificed to a dragon, conquers the dragon, and ends up marrying the princess.

—. *The Persian Cinderella*. Illus. Robert Florczak. New York: HarperCollins, 1999. 32 p. This version is full of the food, customs, culture, and art of Persia. Florczak's note says that he consulted with Persians for authenticity in the intricate, geometric patterns and other art. Settareh's stepsisters are jealous of her beauty. They are invited to Prince Mehrdad's party. Settareh's father gives each girl money with which to buy cloth for a new gown. Settareh spends hers on almonds to eat, on helping a beggar woman, and on a blue jar. The blue jar contains a fairy that grants her wishes. Though her family does not allow her to attend the party, she goes and sees the prince in passing. She hurries home and loses a jeweled anklet. The queen tries the anklet on all the girls in the area, to find that it fits Settareh. The queen introduces Settareh to the prince. He proposes, and the marriage is arranged. The stepsisters are more jealous than ever and break the blue jar. Six hairpins fall out, which the stepsisters shove into Settareh's head. She turns into a dove and flies away to the prince, who befriends her. He discovers the pins beneath the bird's feathers, removes them, and restores Settareh. They marry, and the stepsisters' hearts burst with jealousy, making them explode.

Daly, Jude. *Fair, Brown & Trembling: An Irish Cinderella Story*. Reprint ed. New York: Farrar, 2000. 32 p. Trembling is the name of the Cinderella character. She is held captive in the house because her stepsisters are jealous of her beauty, and Trembling is not allowed to accompany them to church. The Henwife gives her a proper dress and horse to go to church, with the caution that she not step inside. She does this twice, and everyone stares at her. The third week, the men pursue her as she rides away, and the Prince of Emania pulls off a slipper. When he finds that the slipper fits Trembling, the princes fight for her for four days. The Prince of Emania wins and he and Trembling marry. The stepmother and stepsisters were put out to sea in a barrel and were never seen again.

de la Paz, Myrna J. *Abadeha: The Philippine Cinderella*. Illus. Youshan Tang. Auburn, CA: Shen's, 2001. 32 p. Abadeha, a girl living in the Philippines, is mistreated by her jealous stepmother and stepsisters while her father is away. Every time the stepmother challenges her, Abadeha's Spirit of the Forest helps her complete the task. After several incidents, Abadeha fears for her life. The Spirit tells her to plant her dead chicken's feet at her ancestor's grave. A magic tree springs up covered with jewels. A prince finds the tree and takes a ring that squeezes his finger so that he cannot remove it. His father says that the woman who can remove the ring will become the prince's bride. Abadeha removes the ring. She and the prince wed and live happily ever after. The stepmother and stepsisters spend the rest of their lives in the chicken yard. An author note explains the story's background and Filipino traits. The colorful, tropical illustrations add to the story's Philippine feel.

de Paola, Tomie. *Adelita: A Mexican Cinderella Story*. New York: Putnam, 2002. 40 p. This story is set in a Mexican village and sprinkled with Spanish phrases, with a glossary at the end. de Paola's artwork imitates the bright colors and tiles of Mexico. Adelita's father marries a woman with two daughters. Esperanza, the housekeeper, stays on to care for the household, upset that stepmother Micaela favors her own daughters over Adelita. When Adelita's father dies, Micaela treats Adelita cruelly, and her daughters are hateful toward her. Adelita stays in the kitchen with Esperanza until Micaela fires her and orders Adelita to do all of the housework. Micaela and her daughters are invited to a party where the rancher's son will be seeking a wife. Adelita longs to go, as she was acquainted with the son when they were children. Of course, she is not allowed and has to help the others prepare. After the stepmother and sisters go to the fiesta, Esperanza comes by. She finds Adelita's mother's clothes for Adelita to wear and a cart to take her to the fiesta. She introduces herself as Cenicinta, Cinderella. Javier, the son, is in love and dances with her all night. At midnight, when Javier proclaims his love, Adelita panics and runs home. Though there is no glass slipper, Javier searches every house for his Cenicinta. Adelita hangs her mother's shawl out the window, and then helps her sisters dress. Javier sees the shawl and goes to the house. The sisters tell him no one else is there, but Adelita comes out dressed in her fiesta clothes. She tells Javier who she is, and he remembers her from childhood. He still wants to marry her, and Micaela gives her permission. They invite everyone to the wedding, and Esperanza takes care of them. They live happily ever after.

Goode, Diane. *Cinderella: The Dog and Her Little Glass Slipper*. New York: Blue Sky, 2000. 40 p. This retelling follows the traditional Perrault tale except that all the characters are dogs. Some text uses canine phrases, but the real fun comes from the illustrations. In the end, the stepmother and stepsisters beg for forgiveness, which Cinderella grants. She invites them to her wedding because she has the "wisdom of kindness." For younger students.

Hughes, Shirley. *Ella's Big Chance: A Jazz-Age Cinderella*. New York: Simon, 2004. 48 p. Hughes's illustrations give marvelous examples of 1920's fashions and settings. Ella Cinder's father is a tailor and dressmaker, and Ella learns his trade. Buttons, who chats with Ella as she works, works for them as a delivery boy. Mr. Cinders marries a fashionable woman with two stylish daughters. Ella's stepmother becomes the shop manager, and her stepsisters become models. They treat Ella badly, but Buttons is always there to cheer her. The whole family is invited to a ball for the Duke of Arc, but, of course, Ella is not allowed to go. Ella sews dresses for her stepfamily and helps them prepare for the event. After they leave, Buttons invites her for bacon and eggs. Then Ella's fairy godmother appears. She turns Button's bike into a limo and his cat into a chauffeur. She gives Ella a new dress and glass slippers. Buttons is left alone. At the ball, the Duke is smitten with Ella, who dashes out at midnight, leaving a slipper behind. The Duke searches for the shoe's owner and proposes when he finds Ella. She declines in favor of Buttons. Ella and Buttons marry and start their own dress shop.

Jackson, Ellen B. *Cinder Edna*. Illus. Kevin O'Malley. New York: HarperCollins, 1994. 32 p. This version emphasizes the importance of a positive attitude in dealing with life's challenges. Two neighbor girls are each forced to work for their wicked stepfamilies. Ella focuses on her troubles, while Edna makes the best of things by singing, whistling, and learning. Ella is pretty; Edna is not, but Edna is strong and spunky. Ella's fairy godmother dresses her for the ball and gives her transportation. Edna earns money for a dress and takes the bus. Prince Randolph is taken with Ella. Meanwhile, Edna makes herself at home and, finding the prince boring, hits it off with the prince's nerdy brother, Rupert. Both girls leave at midnight, with both princes chasing them. One loafer and one glass slipper are left behind. Randolph searches every foot in the kingdom, while Rupert applies logic and looks in the phone book. They both find their girls and marry them in a double wedding ceremony. Ella is bored with royal life, but Rupert and Edna enjoy life together and live happily ever after.

Jaffe, Nina. *The Way Meat Loves Salt*. Illus. Louise August. New York: Holt, 1998. 32 p. This Jewish Cinderella story begins with a Yiddish pronunciation guide and an author's note about the history of this Jewish version. It ends with the music and words for the song, "Mazel Tov!" A rabbi, his wife, and three daughters live in a small Polish town. The older two girls have gifts of sewing and music. The youngest daughter, Mireleh, has no special gift, yet she is her father's favorite. The rabbi asks his daughters how much they love him. The eldest says, "As much as diamonds." The middle daughter says, "As much as gold and silver." Mireleh says, "The way meat loves salt." The rabbi is so angry by Mireleh's answer that he sends her away forever. A stranger appears to Mireleh and tells her to go to Rabbi Yitskhok's home. He gives her a magic stick that, when tapped three times, will provide whatever Mireleh wishes for. Rabbi Yitskhok takes Mireleh in, where she stays in the attic. When the Rabbi and his family leave to go to a wedding, Mireleh uses the magic stick, which provides garments suitable for a wedding and transportation. She arrives in time for the celebration, and everyone wonders who the lovely maiden is. Rabbi Yitskhok's son dances with her, but she doesn't eat or speak with him. The son paints the front steps with tar where Mireleh's satin slipper gets stuck as she leaves. Her magic stick takes her back to Rabbi Yitskhok's home. The rabbi's son finds the slipper and vows to marry its owner. The rabbi and his wife have the same dream that their son must keep his promise. Mireleh tells the rabbi's son that things are not what they seem and uses the magic stick to conjure fine clothes for him and her. He agrees to marry her. Mireleh orders the cooks for her wedding feast not to put any salt in the food. At the wedding celebration, a visiting rabbi complains about the lack of salt. Mireleh reminds him of what she said to him and how he drove her from his home. He recognizes his daughter and faints. The entire family is reunited when he understands the truth of her saying. The old man who had given Mireleh the magic stick appears and is recognized as the prophet Elijah. The newlyweds live contentedly. Mireleh shares her magic stick with her two daughters, teaching us that the blessings of Elijah stay with us as long as we care for others.

Levine, Gail Carson. *Ella Enchanted*. New York: HarperTrophy, 1997. 232 p. In this fantasy, a Newbery Award winner, Ella is cursed at birth and must obey any command she's given. This leads to some dangerous situations, as well as some funny ones. Ella still mourns her dead mother and resents her often-absent merchant father. When he remarries, his wife and her daughters take advantage of Ella and her curse. Ella's fairy godmother helps her as much as she can, but she cannot reverse the spell. Ella searches for the fairy that cursed her. Along the way, she asserts her intelligence, wit, compassion, and courage to fight enemies and save the prince and the kingdom. Her self-sacrifice breaks her spell, allowing her and the prince to live happily together.

Lowell, Susan. *Cindy Ellen: A Wild Western Cinderella*. Illus. Jane Manning. Reprint ed. New York: HarperTrophy, 2001. 40 p. This tale contains fun Western expressions and details, including a back page of Western lore, mostly about cowgirls. The rancher's daughter, Cindy Ellen, is a good cowgirl but is ill treated by her stepmother and stepsisters. When a big cattle rancher hosts a rodeo and square dance, Cindy's fairy godmother, a little old lady with a golden pistol, dresses her and empowers her: "Magic is plumb worthless without gumption." Cindy meets Joe Prince at the rodeo, where she wins every event. She rushes off, leaving behind a diamond-studded spur. Joe searches and eventually finds its owner. Joe and Cindy marry, and the stepsisters marry city slickers.

Martin, Rafe. *The Rough-Face Girl*. Illus. David Shannon. New York: Putnam, 1992. 32 p. The author's note says, "One way in which the universal yearning for justice has been kept alive is by the many tales of Cinderella." In this version, set in an Indian village on the shores of Lake Ontario, women try to correctly answer the questions asked by the Invisible Being's sister so they can marry the Invisible Being. Only Rough-Face girl, named for facial scars caused by fire cinders, correctly answers the questions. In spite of her appearance, the Invisible Being and his sister declare her beautiful.

Mitchell, Marianne. *Joe Cinders*. Illus. Bryan Langdo. New York: Holt, 2002. 48 p. Joe is the male protagonist in this cowboy Cinderella version. Joe wishes he could go to the costume ball like his wicked stepbrothers. They hope to take over the ranch and win the hand of Rosalinda. Joe's godfather, a "fella with baggy old overalls, a wool serape, and a crooked stick in his hand," gives him a fancy cowboy costume and a red pickup, and turns prairie dogs into cowboys to watch the herd. At a costume ball, the bull gets out. Joe's stepbrothers do nothing to help, but Joe lassos the bull, making him a hero to Rosalinda. He leaves his boot behind as he hurries to leave. Rosalinda finds that he fits the boot. They marry and employ the stepbrothers. The cartoon-like illustrations enhance the rollicking spirit of the text.

Napoli, Donna Jo. *Bound*. New York: Atheneum, 2004. 186 p. This novel for upper elementary and YA girls reveals life and customs in Ming Dynasty China, where foot binding among proper young women is common. The book shows the old values of beauty, wisdom, art, poetry, virtue, family, and reverence of ancestors. Xing-Xing's dead mother gives her courage to get medicine for her stepsister and provides her with fine clothes for a festival. She meets the prince but despises him because she thinks he's shallow. She finds out that he is clever, likes puns, and likes to travel, just as she does. A postscript at the end gives a brief history of "Cinderella."

Palazzo-Craig, Janet. *Tam's Slipper: A Story from Vietnam*. Illus. Makiko Nagano. Mahwah, NJ: Troll, 1996. 32 p. Yellow and orange permeate the text and art of this Cinderella version. Tam lives with her stepmother and stepsister. Tam does all the work, and her stepsister, Cam, gets all the credit. A beautiful woman dressed in yellow and orange appears and tells her that she will be rewarded for being strong and kind. Tam finds a yellow and orange fish in her basket. She keeps it in her pond. A rooster with yellow and orange feathers shows up, and the horse's coat shines yellow and orange. The prince comes for the harvest festival. Before Tam can go to the festival, she must husk an enormous cart of rice. Her animal friends help her husk and provide her with festival clothing and transportation. She loses one of her slippers at the festival, which the prince finds. He searches for its owner, finds Tam, and falls in love with her.

San Souci, Robert D. *Cendrillon: A Caribbean Cinderella*. Illus. Brian Pinkney. New York: Simon, 1998. 40 p. Told from the grandmother's point of view, this tale evokes the rhythms, customs, flora, and fauna of the Caribbean. The text is peppered with French Creole phrases, which are not always explained in the text but are defined in a glossary. This Cinderella has a magic wand given to her by her dying mother, but when her Paul finds her, she asks grandmother to remove the magic so he can see her as she really is. He still loves her and they marry, hosting a fabulous wedding feast.

—-. *Cinderella Skeleton*. Illus. David Catrow. San Diego: Silver Whistle/Harcourt, 2000. 32 p. This rhyming tale with an all-skeleton cast has Cinderella seeking someone who loves dirt as much as she does. She finds him in the prince at his ball. Her foot snaps off and is left behind as she runs away, but the prince finds the right bone match. "You make each day a Halloween," he says. The stepmother and stepsisters shrivel to dust.

—-. *Little Gold Star: A Spanish American Cinderella Tale*. Illus. Sergio Martinez. New York: HarperCollins, 2000. 32 p. Set in New Mexico with sheepherder characters, the Virgin Mary blesses Teresa for her goodness and curses the stepdaughters for their meanness. With the Virgin Mary's help, Teresa completes impossible tasks her stepmother requires before Teresa can marry a rich rancher. The stepmother and sisters grow kinder, and all live happily ever after.

—-. *Sootface: An Ojibwa Cinderella Story*. New York: Doubleday, 1994. 32 p. This Ojibwa version is similar to Rafe Martin's *Rough-Face Girl*. Set in the Great Lakes area, a mighty warrior asks his sister to find him a wife with a kind and honest heart. The sister vets the candidates by asking questions. No one answers correctly until Sootface, so named because of her fire-scarred, dirty face. The warrior and Sootface marry, and the stepsisters must do their own chores.

Sanderson, Ruth. *Cinderella*. Boston: Little, 2002. 32 p. Lush, realistic oil illustrations depict French court and manor scenes. The text is based on the Perrault version, with some of the Grimms' details, such as aid from the white bird. At the end the stepmother and stepsisters repent and Cinderella forgives them. However, birds peck the stepmother and stepsister until they flee into the house where the birds guard them so they can never go out.

Schroeder, Alan. *Smoky Mountain Rose: An Appalachian Cinderella*. Illus. Brad Sneed. New York: Dial, 1997. 32 p. An author's note gives background on "Cinderella." This version is based on Perrault's but takes place in the Smoky Mountains. The dialogue is written in mountain dialect. Father is a trapper who marries a widow with two daughters. They are all mean and vain, but Rose remains sweet and caring. Father dies. When a rich feller gives a party, the hog helps Rose attend by dressing her well, changing mice into horses and watermelon into a wagon, and giving her glass slippers. Her stepsisters recognize her at the party, but the rich man falls for her. Rose runs out at midnight, leaving a shoe behind. Just before her stepsisters start beating her, the rich feller shows up with her shoe. It fits her, and she marries the feller. She forgives her stepfamily and they give her no more trouble. The illustrations are like images in a fun-house mirror, stretched in unusual ways in the style of Thomas Hart Benton.

Sierra, Judy. *The Gift of the Crocodile: A Cinderella Story*. Illus. Reynold Ruffins. New York: Simon, 2000. 40 p. This Indonesian version tells how Damura remembered her dead mother's teaching to respect all wild creatures. When her stepmother and stepsisters treat her cruelly, the crocodiles help her. They bring her clothing to wear to the prince's ball, where she leaves a slipper behind. When the prince finds her and proposes, Damura's step relatives take her on a boat ride and push her overboard. A crocodile swallows her. The prince calls on Grandmother Crocodile, who forces the young crocodile to spit Damura up. Grandmother Crocodile brings Damura back to life, and tells the young crocodiles to eat up the step relatives. The step relatives overhear and run away. The book contains a folklore note. The illustrations show prints of Indonesian fabric, colors, flora, and fauna.

Steptoe, John. *Mufaro's Beautiful Daughters: An African Tale*. Lothrop, 1987. 32 p. Mufaro lives in an African village with his two beautiful daughters. Manyara is bad-tempered, while Nyasha is known for kindness. Nyasha sings as she works and befriends a snake in her garden. The family receives an invitation from the king, who is looking for a wife. Manyara sets out at night so she can reach the king first. She refuses to help a hungry boy in her path and comes upon an old woman who gives her advice. Manyara is rude and ignores the advice. Nyasha awakes to cries of villagers searching for the missing Manyara. When they find her footprints heading toward the city, they go on. Nyasha feeds the hungry boy her sister would not help. The old woman who advised Manyara appears to Nyasha and points the right way. Nyasha thanks her with a gift of sunflower seeds. She is awestruck when she sees the city for the first time. As they enter the city, Manyara runs out from a chamber, crying in fear. She warns them not to continue, but Nyasha goes on. Instead of the monster Manyara warns against, Nyasha finds her friend, the snake. He changes shape to become the king. He has also been the hungry boy and the old woman. He recognizes Nyasha's kindness and asks her to marry him. Mufaro proudly proclaims his pride for his daughter, Nyasha, the queen, and his other daughter, Manyara, the queen's servant. Beautiful realistic paintings enhance this winner of the Coretta Scott King Award for Illustrator and Caldecott Honor Book.

Thomas, Joyce Carol. *The Gospel Cinderella*. Illus. David Diaz. New York: Amistad, 2004. 40 p. Queen Mother Rhythm's baby was snatched away in a hurricane. She and the Great Gospel Choir keep singing and looking for the baby. Meanwhile, the baby lands in the clutches of a wicked Foster Mother and twin girls. When Queen Mother announces her impending retirement and advertises open auditions for vocalist, all the girls in the swamp try out. Cinderella sings from behind the brush, and Queen Mother recognizes her daughter. Cinderella becomes Daughter of Rhythm and sings a duet with the Prince of Music, with whom she goes on to lead the Great Gospel Choir. Set in the South, this tale contains poetic language and a joyful tone.

Whipple, Laura. *If the Shoe Fits: Voices from Cinderella*. Illus. Laura Beingessner. New York: McElderry, 2002. 67 p. This book contains 33 free verse poems including voices from all the Cinderella characters, including the glass slipper. The poems are arranged with a prelude, the sequential story as told in poetry by Cinderella's father's ghost, the stepmother, the cat, the king, and others, ending with a coda. This collection for older students will help them see the story in new ways and understand the literary concept of point of view.

Rapunzel

Themes
- Maturation
- Selfishness
- Keeping promises
- Making bargains
- The nature of true love
- What other themes can you and your students find?

In most versions of "Rapunzel," the main character's name is a type of herb or vegetable. "Rapunzel" means "rampion," a German salad vegetable. The Italian "Petrosinella," written by Giambattista Basile in 1687, comes from their word for "parsley," as does the French version's "Persinette," written by Charlotte Rose de Caumont de la Force in 1697. In fact, several others translated the tale from French into German before the Grimms. The Grimms' versions most closely resemble that of translator J.C.F. Schulz, who changed "Persinette" to "Rapunzel."

The best-known version of "Rapunzel" comes to us from the Grimm brothers. Jacob wrote the first version published in 1812, and Wilhelm wrote a slightly different version published in 1857. (A detailed comparison of differences between these versions is found at D. L. Ashliman's *Rapunzel* Web site.) The tale was known in other countries long before the Grimms wrote it down, however.

The AT Index classifies this story as a "Maiden in a Tower" type. Plot and characters vary among versions. Some contain a fairy, some a witch, some a sorceress. Some versions separate the main character and the prince for years before they are reunited. Some have the main character and the prince elope. Versions other than the Grimms' contain humor, usually in the form of silly magic, such as a tattletale saucepan.

Sources Consulted

Aarne, Antti. *The Types of the Folktale, a Classification and Bibliography*. Helsinki, Finland: Suomalainen Tiedeakatemia, 1961.
Ashliman, D. L. *Rapunzel*. 22 Jun. 2006. 02 June 2007 <www.pitt.edu/~dash/grimm012a.html>.
Bettelheim, Bruno. *Uses of Enchantment*. New York: Knopf, 1977.
Heiner, Heidi Anne. "History of Rapunzel." *SurLaLune Fairy Tales*. 12 Nov. 2002. 02 June 2007 <www.surlalunefairytales.com/rapunzel/history.html>.
Lüthi, Max. *The Fairytale as Art Form and Portrait of Man*. Bloomington: Indiana UP, 1984.
—-. *Once Upon a Time: On the Nature of Fairy Tales*. Bloomington: Indiana UP, 1976.
Zipes, Jack. *Breaking the Magic Spell: Radical Theories of Folk and Fairy Tales*. Austin: U of Texas P, 1979.
—-. *When Dreams Came True: Classical Fairy Tales and Their Tradition*. New York: Routledge, 1999.

Selected Annotated Bibliography

Berenzy, Alix. *Rapunzel*. Reprint ed. New York: Holt, 1998. 32 p. Berenzy bases her retelling on the original Grimm version. The book begins with a definition of "rapunzel," a salad green. This green is craved by a pregnant woman whose husband steals it from the garden next door owned by the ancient fairy, Mother Gothel. In exchange for the rapunzel, the husband agrees to give their child to Mother Gothel when it is born. When the baby is born, Mother Gothel names her Rapunzel and takes her away. When the girl turns 12, Mother Gothel puts her in a tower, which Mother Gothel accesses via Rapunzel's long golden hair. Rapunzel sings to stave off loneliness. A prince hears her sweet voice and longs to meet her. He observes Mother Gothel's method and tries it himself. Rapunzel pulls him up on her hair, the first man she's ever seen. He proposes to her, and she agrees to marry him if he will visit her every day and bring a skein of silk that she will weave into a ladder. She cautions him to come only in the evening. They go along until Rapunzel gives her secret away to Mother Gothel, who cuts Rapunzel's hair and sends her away alone to the desert. Mother Gothel waits for the prince and pulls him up on Rapunzel's hair. He jumps from the window and falls into a thorn bush, blinding him. He wanders in the wilderness. After years, he hears a sweet voice and hurries toward it. It is Rapunzel singing to her twins, a boy and a girl. She recognizes him and runs to him. The tears from her eyes fall into his, restoring his sight. They are thankful to be together and take their family back to his kingdom where they are welcomed and live happily ever after. The lush illustrations use glowing focal light to emphasize mood and detail.

Grimm, Jacob and Wilhelm Grimm. *Rapunzel*. Illus. Felix Hoffmann. New York: Harcourt, 1964. n. pag. This version, accompanied by Swiss artist, Hoffmann's stark, dark drawings, has a witch as the owner of the rapunzel garden. The agreement, rapunzel for the unborn baby, is made. The witch collects the baby when she is born and names her Rapunzel, locking her in a tower when she turns 12.

The witch gets to the tower on Rapunzel's long golden hair. A prince hears Rapunzel sing and wants to meet her. He sees how the witch gets to the tower and tries it himself. He proposes, and she says yes but needs him to bring a length of silk to weave into a ladder so she can escape. Rapunzel gives her secret away to the witch accidentally. She cuts off Rapunzel's hair and uses it to lure the prince. He falls into thorns and is blinded. Rapunzel sees and hears what happens and jumps out the window after him. When she finds the prince, her tears fall into his eyes, restoring his sight. They go to his kingdom where they live happily ever after. The witch, however, is stuck in the tower and shrivels to the size of an apple. A bird picks her up to take to its nest as food for its babies.

Grimm, Jacob, and Wilhelm Grimm. *Rapunzel: A Fairy Tale*. Trans. Anthea Bell. Illus. Maja Dusíková. New York: North-South, 1997. 32 p. Soft watercolor illustrations set the scene in medieval Western Europe. The husband takes rapunzel from the neighbor's garden to thwart his pregnant wife's cravings. The witch who owns the garden bargains with him, her rapunzel for his child when it is born. She takes the daughter and names her Rapunzel. When she turns 12, Rapunzel is put in a tower from which she can't escape. The witch climbs into the tower on Rapunzel's long golden hair. A passing prince hears Rapunzel sing and wants to meet her. He sees how the witch gets into the tower and tries it himself at dusk. He asks Rapunzel to marry him, and she agrees but asks him to bring silk cords with him from which she will make a ladder. He does, but before they can elope, Rapunzel lets her secret slip to the witch, who cuts her hair and sends her to live in a deserted part of the forest. The prince climbs Rapunzel's hair and meets the witch. He jumps out the window and is blinded by thorns. He wanders through the forest for years until he hears Rapunzel singing. She recognizes him, weeps over him, and restores his eyesight. He takes Rapunzel home to his kingdom where they live happily ever after.

Harris, Marian. *Rapunzel*. Illus. Jim Harris. Denver, CO: Accord, 1995. 32 p. Jim Harris's outrageous witch and dark artwork full of hidden details will delight children and make them squeal. Marian Harris's retelling is dramatic, using dialogue to move the story and show emotion. She describes scenes from a child's point of view, such as Rapunzel's tea party with Mouse and Badger. This version's witch is mean and does not allow Rapunzel to have friends of any species, locking her in a tower. The witch climbs up the tower on Rapunzel's long hair and brings her food. Rapunzel's friends, Mouse and Badger, keep her company and bring her fresh strawberries. When a prince passes by and hears Rapunzel sing, he wants to meet her. He sees how the witch gains access and tries it himself. He falls in love with Rapunzel, and she tells him how she became imprisoned. The prince brings her yarn and knitting needles so that she can make a ladder. Rapunzel lets her secret slip to the witch, who cuts off Rapunzel's hair and sends her away to the Northern Wild. When the prince ascends Rapunzel's hair, he meets the witch, who tosses him down into thorns that blind him. Badger leads the prince in search of Rapunzel. When they find her, she cries, and her tears restore the prince's sight. They marry and live happily ever after, with Mouse and Badger, in the prince's kingdom.

Roberts, Lynn. *Rapunzel: A Groovy Fairy Tale*. Illus. David Roberts. New York: Abrams, 2003. 32 p. This Rapunzel lives in the 1970's and has long red hair. She lives with her Aunt Esme and Roach, Esme's pet crow. Esme keeps Rapunzel locked up. Esme gets up and down from her apartment on Rapunzel's hair, since the elevator is always broken. A boy sees this happen and recognizes Esme as the cafeteria lady. He calls for Rapunzel to let down her hair, and soon she is face-to-face with Roger. They spend the morning listening to music and talking. Roger visits every day after Esme leaves the apartment. They make a rope ladder from scarves and belts. Rapunzel errs and lets slip to Esme that she has been pulling Roger up, enraging Esme. She cuts off Rapunzel's hair and sends her down. Esme pulls Roger up on Rapunzel's hair, to his horror. Esme pushes him off the balcony, where he falls unconscious. Rapunzel roams the city, lost and hungry, longing for Roger. Roger's head injury affects his memory, and he does not remember Rapunzel. Rapunzel sees a poster for Roger's band's concert. She gets a seat in the front row, and when he sees her, he remembers. They become best friends, Roger's band becomes very successful, and Rapunzel goes into the wig making business. Esme is left to walk up and down the stairs in and out of her apartment. Grotesque cartoon illustrations with plenty of teen flair add to the story.

Zelinsky, Paul O. *Rapunzel*. New York: Dutton, 1997. 48 p. Zelinsky emphasizes this story's Italian and French roots with his rich oil paintings reminiscent of Italian masters. Renaissance scenes depict cypress, courtyards, red tile roofs, Roman ruins, and finely woven carpets. An author note at the end gives a brief history of "Rapunzel." The tale begins with a couple joyfully accepting the wife's pregnancy. When she craves the herb rapunzel from the neighbor's garden, her husband obliges by stealing some. This only makes her want more. When the husband returns to the garden, the sorceress who owns the garden bargains with him. He may take the rapunzel if they give her their child. When their daughter is born, the sorceress appears in the room, names the baby Rapunzel, and takes her. When the girl turns 12, the sorceress puts her in a tower. The sorceress visits Rapunzel by climbing up and down on Rapunzel's long red-gold hair. Rapunzel lives this way for years until a prince rides by and hears her singing. He longs to meet her and observes the sorceress's access to the tower. He calls for Rapunzel to let down her hair, and he climbs up. Rapunzel is upset, as she has never seen a man before, but he speaks kindly and assuages her fear. He proposes marriage, and she accepts. They hold a ceremony in the tower, and the prince visits every night. The sorceress discovers the truth when Rapunzel asks for help fastening her too-tight dress. The sorceress cuts off Rapunzel's hair and sends her to live alone in the wilderness. Here, Rapunzel gives birth to twins, a boy and a girl. When the prince calls for Rapunzel at the tower, the sorceress lets Rapunzel's hair down. He climbs up and is confronted by the angry sorceress. He lets go of the hair and falls to the ground. Blinded in the fall, he wanders the wilderness, eating roots and berries. One day he hears Rapunzel's voice, and they are happily reunited. When they embrace, her tears fall into his eyes, restoring his sight. The prince leads his family to his kingdom where they live happily ever after.

Sleeping Beauty

> **Themes**
> - Maturation
> - Death and resurrection
> - Beauty
> - The power of love
> - What other themes can you and your students find?

A beautiful princess cursed by a fairy has been resting for hundreds of years as Brynhild, Briar Rose, Aurora, or Sleeping Beauty. A Norse story about Brynhild from the mid-1300's may have provided the seed for the first "Sleeping Beauty." A text from France's 1500's, *Perceforest*, is a more substantial source, with yet a fuller version in Italian by Basile in 1636. France's Perrault's version followed in 1697. Perrault's story, published in English in 1729, gained popularity as a separate chapbook (a small, inexpensive paperback book). The story was often performed in pantomime. The Grimm brothers published their version, "Dornröschen" ("Briar Rose") in the early 1800's. Both the Perrault and the Grimm versions are well-known in the U.S.

The AT Index classifies "Sleeping Beauty" as one of the tales of "Supernatural or Enchanted Husband (Wife) or Other Relatives." Friederich Vogt, an essayist, wrote in 1896 that the Grimm, Perrault, and Basile versions originated in myths about the seasons, with Sleeping Beauty's awakening representing spring (McGlathery 72-73). The Italian and French versions contained gruesome scenes and violent endings including cannibalism, murder or attempted murder, and suicide. The Grimm version and most modern versions omit the violence and are more suitable for children. The Grimm version and most modern versions end with the prince waking Sleeping Beauty with a kiss. Other versions include the first years of the prince and Sleeping Beauty's married life.

Sources Consulted

Aarne, Antti. *The Types of the Folktale, a Classification and Bibliography*. Helsinki, Finland: Suomalainen Tiedeakatemia, 1961.

Bettelheim, Bruno. *Uses of Enchantment*. New York: Knopf, 1977.

Heiner, Heidi Anne. "History of Sleeping Beauty." *SurLaLune Fairy Tales*. 16 May 2007. 02 June 2007 <www.surlalunefairytales.com/sleepingbeauty/history.html>.

McGlathery, James M. *Grimms' Fairy Tales: A History of Criticism on a Popular Classic*. Columbia, SC: Camden, 1993.

Opie, Iona and Peter Opie. *The Classic Fairy Tales*. New York: Oxford UP, 1974.

Selected Annotated Bibliography

Craft, Mahlon F. *Sleeping Beauty*. Illus. K. Y. Craft. New York: SeaStar, 2002. 32 p. This retelling and its illustrations make this book a true work of art. The retelling is quite traditional. However, an untraditional part of the story is when the rest of the court falls asleep with Aurora, but not the king and queen who had been out, and behold their daughter's fate. The twelfth fairy that gave the 100 years sleep spell comes and comforts them, and then puts them to sleep, too. The prince who finds her does so from the noble motivation that a beautiful princess should not be lying among thorns unprotected. After the prince and princess marry, they become known around the realm for their good and kindly deeds. The soft, romantic illustrations contain a golden glow, and include an illuminated manuscript look on the text pages.

Horosko, Marian. *Sleeping Beauty: The Ballet Story*. Illus. Todd L. W. Doney. New York: Atheneum, 1994. 32 p. A narrative description of the ballet version of this story accompanies ballet scene illustrations based on the Perrault story version, Marius Petipa's choreography, and Tchaikovsky's music. The main characters have names, including Sleeping Beauty, Aurora. The text includes music and curtain cues, as well as stage entrances and exits.

Keller, Emily Snowell. *Sleeping Bunny*. Illus. Pamela Silin-Palmer. New York: Random, 2003. 34 p. Vivid illustrations of animal characters, including pig butterflies and other woodland creatures, decorate this tale whose main cast of characters are rabbits. Because Fairy Mildew was not invited to Princess Bunny's christening, Mildew cursed the bunny. When Princess Bunny pricks her finger and falls asleep according to the curse, a young Rabbit Prince rescues her one hundred years later. Having learned their lesson, they invite all the fairies, including Mildew, to their wedding feast.

Lasky, Kathryn. *Humphrey, Albert, and the Flying Machine*. Illus. John Manders. Orlando, FL: Harcourt, 2004. 40 p. This story is loosely based on "Sleeping Beauty" and the life of historical figure Daniel Bernoulli, a European inventor in the 1700's. Humphrey and Albert are the first to awaken at Briar Rose's party after 100 years sleep. The boys hack their way out of the palace and seek a prince to kiss the princess, which will awaken the rest of the court. They find handsome noblemen too boring, but then they happen upon Daniel and his flying machine. Together, they fly it to the palace, Daniel kisses the princess, and the boys grow up to be inventors. An author note gives brief factual information about Bernoulli.

Levine, Gail Carson. *Princess Sonora and the Long Sleep*. New York: HarperCollins, 1999. 107 p. One of Levine's "Princess Tales" series, this book is billed for grades two through seven. Levine humorously twists the traditional Sleeping Beauty plot. At her christening, in addition to being given the curse of being pricked by a spindle, Princess Sonora is given the gift of being ten times smarter than anyone else. She likes to think and show off her brains, though her reasoning is not often sound by our standards. She is disappointed that no one wants to listen to her. This saying becomes a proverb in her kingdom: Princess Sonora knows, but don't ask her. After her court's hundred-year sleep, Prince Christopher arrives to break the spell, fighting his way through decades of dirt and cobwebs. The prince is always wondering why, and he has finally met the person who can tell him. They marry and live happily ever after.

Osborne, Will and Mary Pope Osborne. *Sleeping Bobby*. Illus. Giselle Potter. New York: Atheneum, 2005. 40 p. A gender reversal has Baby Bob born to royal parents and receiving a curse that he would prick his finger on a spindle when he turns 18 and die. Instead of death, the curse is altered to 100 years' sleep. Bob grows up to be kind, clever, modest, handsome, and admired. Though spindles are destroyed, Bob finds one and enacts the curse. A princess finds the kingdom just as the 100 years is past. She is allowed to enter the thorn hedge, finds Bob, and kisses him. They immediately fall in love and are married. Amusing child-like illustrations accompany the text.

Yolen, Jane. *Sleeping Ugly*. Illus. Diane Stanley. New York: Putnam, 1981. 64 p. Princess Miserella is beautiful outside, but mean and worthless inside. In the same kingdom, orphan Plain Jane was not beautiful outside, but was kind and good. When Miserella gets lost in the forest, she finds a fairy disguised as an old woman who leads her to Jane's house. Miserella behaves miserably, and the fairy casts spells on her that Jane, who has been given three wishes, wishes undone. In a magic wand accident, they are all put to sleep for 100 years. Prince Jojo, who has no property or money, comes along to break the spell. He practices kissing the fairy first, then Jane. They awake before Jojo kisses Miserella. He sees that she is pretty outside and ugly inside, as he has cousins like that. He marries Jane. He fixes up their cottage and builds a house next door for the fairy. Miserella sleeps on in their home and no one, not even their three children, are allowed to kiss her awake.

Beauty and the Beast

Themes
- Internal and external beauty
- Virtue
- Self-sacrifice
- Treatment of those who are different
- Appropriate female and male roles in relationships
- Goals and motivations
- Selfishness
- Vanity
- Greed
- What other themes can you and your students find?

Beauty is known not only for her good looks, but also for her virtue and self-sacrifice. She is depicted as truly beautiful inside and out.

Usually, folktales and fairy tales are told orally and then are written down to become literary tales. Some scholars speculate that "Beauty and the Beast" as we know it took the opposite process. They think it began as a literary tale that was told so frequently it became part of the oral folk tradition (Heiner, "History of Beauty").

The Opies declare "Beauty and the Beast" the most symbolic fairy tale after "Cinderella," and the most intellectually satisfying (179). It is a classic example of the beast marriage story, which has variations around the world. The AT Index classifies "Beauty and the Beast" as a subtype of "The Search for the Lost Husband," which shares these features: the monster is the husband, a girl promises to marry the monster, and the girl disenchants the monster with affection. Elements of the story occur as far back as Greek mythology's *Cupid and Psyche*. Throughout time, these stories have been staged for audiences.

A French woman, Madame Gabrielle Susanne Barbot de Gallon de Villeneuve, wrote a long version of "Beauty and the Beast" in 1740, with her adult salon friends as the intended audience. This was the basis for another French woman's version, published in French in 1756 and in English in 1761. Madame Leprince de Beaumont's version became the standard upon which modern versions are based. Her version was shorter, without subplots, and aimed at young aristocratic ladies between the ages of five and 13 (Griswold 50). It emphasized Beauty's virtue and self-sacrifice.

"Beauty and the Beast" has been presented and studied from seemingly every possible angle and offers readers and audiences deep, universal themes to ponder.

Sources Consulted

Aarne, Antti. *The Types of the Folktale, a Classification and Bibliography*. Helsinki, Finland: Suomalainen Tiedeakatemia, 1961.

Bettelheim, Bruno. *Uses of Enchantment*. New York: Knopf, 1977.

Griswold, Jerry. *The Meanings of "Beauty and the Beast": A Handbook*. Peterborough, Ont.: Broadview, 2004.

Heiner, Heidi Anne. "History of Beauty and the Beast." 3 Nov. 2003. 02 June 2007 <www.surlalunefairytales.com/beautybeast/history.html>.

Opie, Iona and Peter Opie. *The Classic Fairy Tales*. New York: Oxford UP, 1974.

Selected Annotated Bibliography

Brett, Jan. *Beauty and the Beast*. New York: Clarion, 1989. 32 p. Brett's characteristic artwork frames pages and text, creating a demure, yet strong, Beauty, and a refined, elegant boar Beast. Other creatures, such as dogs and monkeys, act as servants. The tale is quite traditional. In this version, Beauty declines to marry Beast, but agrees to live with him forever, but wishes to visit her family to say goodbye. Nothing had changed in her family dynamics, and they do not understand her new life. Still, they keep so busy with social engagements that Beauty forgets her promise to return to the Beast until she sees him in a dream, dying. She goes back immediately and finds him near death in the garden. She declares her love for him and says she will marry him. The Beast turns into a handsome prince. He explains that a fairy had put a curse on his palace and everyone in it because she did not like that people put too much importance on appearances. Beauty breaks the spell when she looks at the Beast's heart and agrees to marry him for who he is rather than how he looks. They marry and live happily ever after.

Hautzig, Deborah. *Beauty and the Beast*. Illus. Kathy Mitchell. New York: Random, 1995. 48 p. This Step into Reading Step 3 Book for second and third graders begins with a note to parents about the series. Pleasant illustrations and sparse text on every page give beginning readers confidence. Though Hautzig uses grade-level vocabulary, she writes well and makes the story exciting. Beauty is good and virtuous, while her sisters are vain and selfish. The story unfolds traditionally. When Beauty and Beast marry, a fairy gives her approval to Beauty and turns her sisters into statues.

Mayer, Marianna. *Beauty and the Beast*. Illus. Mercer Mayer. New York: SeaStar, 2000. 48 p. Mercer Mayer's detailed illustrations set the tale in medieval times and enhance the text. Marianna has added three hard-working brothers to Beauty's family, as well as three vain sisters. The themes of looking beyond the surface and valuing the inner person are clearly brought out as the tale follows the traditional plot. It is Beauty's love that saves her father and breaks the Beast's enchantment.

Willard, Nancy. *Beauty and the Beast*. Illus. Barry Moser. New York: Harcourt, 1992. 69 p. This is appropriate for older children because of the dark woodcut illustrations, amount of narrative text, and sophisticated subjects. This version includes an astrologer who acts as a fortune-teller. Willard sets this retelling in New York, with the merchant's family living in a townhouse overlooking Central Park. When they lose their fortune, they move to the merchant's deceased wife's country cottage. In spite of circumstances and having to do all the hard work at the cottage, Beauty maintains a cheerful demeanor while the rest of the family withers. The merchant hears that one of his ships came in, and he goes to the city to see about it. He purchases expensive items on credit for two of his daughters and then learns that the ship has gone on, the cargo is sold, and he is not a penny richer for it. Dejected, he rides his horse through the icy winter countryside and takes shelter at the Beast's mansion. After enjoying first-class accommodations, he sets out to leave in the morning and picks a rose from the trellis. The Beast becomes unhinged and seeks to punish the merchant but agrees that one of the merchant's daughters may die in the merchant's place. Beauty offers to go, and though afraid, she treats Beast with courtesy. He supplies the apartment of her dreams in which she stays. She teaches Beast to play chess with her and declines his marriage proposal. She dreams of her mother, who is proud of her. Beauty sees that things are not as they seem. Beauty explores the Beast's mansion and finds clues to his real identity. Beauty goes back home to visit her sick father, promising to return in a week. Her selfish sisters foil her intent to keep her promise by lying to her. She discovers their deception and returns to a dying Beast. She proposes marriage to him, and he immediately becomes a handsome young man, the mansion is populated with servants, and her father arrives on the doorstep. Her sisters appear as cast iron wood holders by the fireplace.

Yep, Laurence. *The Dragon Prince: A Chinese Beauty and the Beast Tale*. Illus. Kam Mak. New York: HarperCollins, 1997. 32 p. Seven, the Chinese Beauty, is the youngest, prettiest, and hardest working daughter of a poor farmer. She kindly saves a serpent from being killed by her sister's hoe. The serpent becomes a dragon that asks the farmer for one of his daughters to marry in exchange for the farmer's life. The other daughters run away in fear, but Seven, though afraid, agrees to marry the dragon to save her father. The dragon takes Seven to live with him under the sea. Seven looks at him with wonder, not fear, because she sees him with her heart. When she declares this, the dragon turns into a handsome prince, and he and Seven marry. They live in elegance, but Seven misses her family and goes to visit. Seven's sister, Three, jealous of Seven's finery, switches clothes with her, and pushes her into the river. Three tells the rest of the family what she has done. They send a message to the prince saying that Seven has fallen ill and will be delayed. She may even look different. Three goes to the prince. He doesn't care that she is now ugly but is surprised that she doesn't know where anything is or know how to work the loom at which Seven had been an expert. The prince goes hunting for the truth. Seven does not drown and is taken in by an elderly woman. Seven embroiders shoes for the woman to sell. The prince searches and sees the embroidered shoes. He buys them, follows the woman home, and is reunited with Seven. He becomes a dragon and takes Seven and the woman to his home under the sea. They send Three back to her family and live happily ever after. The illustrations evoke rural and fanciful China beautifully.

Snow White

> **Themes**
> - Parent-child relationships
> - Death and resurrection
> - Loyalty
> - Vengeance
> - Gender roles
> - Maturation
> - Jealousy
> - External and internal beauty
> - What other themes can you and your students find?

Think of Snow White and chances are the Disney image of the fair-skinned, raven-haired princess in blue bodice and yellow skirt comes to mind. While she waits for her prince to come, she keeps house for seven dwarfs and befriends the forest creatures until her evil stepmother tries to kill her with a poisoned apple. Disney's 1937 release of *Snow White*, the first full-length animated feature film, is imprinted on peoples' minds as the real story.

The AT Index gives Snow White its own classification number. It falls under the larger grouping of the "Persecuted Heroine" type and the subgrouping in which the heroine falls into a death-like sleep. Evidence shows that this tale existed across Europe, Asia Minor, and to central Africa. "Snow White" did not come to the Western hemisphere until later, when written versions became available.

In 1634, Basile's *Pentamerone* told a similar tale about a girl named Lisa. As always, versions differ. Disney ended the story with the prince and Snow White riding off to his castle to live happily ever after. The Grimms' version's character is known as Sneewitchen or Snow-Drop, and continues the story to the couple's wedding. There, the evil stepmother is forced to dance in iron shoes that have been heated in a fire until she drops dead.

Disney did not veer from the stepmother's evil motive and inserted a violent scene from a version earlier than the Grimms' version. This version has the queen ask the huntsman to bring back the heart of the dead princess. Disney forgoes the rest of the scene, where the queen eats the boar's heart the huntsman has brought her, thinking she is eating the heart of the dead girl.

In some versions, the evil one is the girl's real mother, while most versions since the Grimms portray an evil stepmother. The dwarfs are not named in most versions. Some versions substitute knights, thieves, robbers, or other beings.

The story has been analyzed from every direction by numerous kinds of scholars for various purposes because it contains many thematic layers to consider.

Sources Consulted

Aarne, Antti. *The Types of the Folktale, a Classification and Bibliography*. Helsinki, Finland: Suomalainen Tiedeakatemia, 1961.

Bettelheim, Bruno. *Uses of Enchantment*. New York: Knopf, 1977.

Heiner, Heidi Anne. "History of Snow White and the Seven Dwarfs." *SurLaLune Fairy Tales*. 12 Nov. 2002. 02 June 2007 <www.surlalunefairytales.com/sevendwarfs/history.html>.

Opie, Iona and Peter Opie. *The Classic Fairy Tales*. New York: Oxford UP, 1974.

Vandergrift, Kay E. *Snow White*. 02 June 2007 <www.scils.rutgers.edu/~kvander/snowwhite.html>.

Selected Annotated Bibliography

Aiken, Joan. *Snow White and the Seven Dwarfs*. Illus. Belinda Downes. New York: DK, 2002. 44 p. Embroidered cloth illustrations give this book a quaint, folksy feeling. In addition to being beautiful, this Snow White is friendly and kind to all. She is loved by everyone but her stepmother, who descended from a long line of witches. The author adds a few humorous lines to the magic mirror's poems to let the stepmother know that her youth and beauty are gone. Most of the dwarfs have ordinary names, such as Fred and Ted. The evil stepmother nearly succeeds in killing Snow White with tight satin laces and a poisoned comb. Finally, she offers a poisoned apple that seems to do the deed. The seemingly dead princess is laid in a glass coffin. The Prince of the Western Isles finds her and dislodges the poison in her throat. She agrees to marry the prince if she can bring the dwarfs along. The evil stepmother's mirror tells her that Snow White is marrying. In a rage, she smashes the mirror. One of the shards pierces her heart and she dies. The rest of the pieces fly back to the mirror's maker, who molds them into a ball. Everyone else lives happily ever after.

Delessert, Etienne. *The Seven Dwarfs*. Mankato, MN: Creative, 2001. 32 p. This Snow White story is told from the point of view of the eldest of the aging seven dwarfs, Stephane, after they return from Snow White's wedding to Prince Gabriel. Stephane tells how Snow White came to live with them and nearly die at the hands of her evil stepmother. In return for saving Snow White's life, the prince dubs the dwarfs "Dukes of the Forest" and offers them a place to live in his kingdom. The dwarfs appreciate a peek at luxury, but decline the offer, happy to live in their forest cottage.

Jarrell, Randall. *Snow-White and the Seven Dwarfs*. Illus. Nancy Ekholm Burkert. New York: Farrar, 1972. 32 p. A Caldecott Honor Book, the pictures accompanying the text are worth sinking into. Many double spreads pace the story with their detail and beauty. Jarrell's retelling is traditional, with the evil queen forced to don fire-heated iron slippers and dance until she drops dead at the end.

Ljungkvist, Laura. *Snow White and the Seven Dwarfs*. New York: Abrams, 2003. 40 p. This Swedish author-illustrator gives an old tale a pop-art look with bright oddly placed colors and graphic images. Snow White's stepmother sends Snow White out in the night hoping wild animals will kill her. Instead, because they love her, they guide her to the home of the seven dwarfs. Ljungkvist condenses the tale and has the stepmother sneak a poisoned apple onto Snow White's plate at the dwarfs' house. When she takes a bite, she instantly falls into a coma. The dwarfs lay her in the garden on a bed of roses. Prince Sunray finds her and shakes her, dislodging the poisoned apple piece. Snow White awakens and accepts Prince Sunray's marriage proposal. When the evil stepmother hears about it, she tries to stop the wedding, but the wild beasts stop her. She is never heard from again, while everyone else lives happily ever after.

Poole, Josephine. *Snow White*. Illus. Angela Barrett. New York: Knopf, 1991. n. pag. Dramatic paintings adorn the text of this story, where the jealous stepmother tries in vain to kill Snow White. In this ending, the prince makes the dwarfs his counselors, and they all live happily ever after, while the evil stepmother dies from her own poisoned rose.

Santore, Charles. *Snow White*. New York: Random, 1997. 48 p. Author-illustrator Santore has created a realistic forest and medieval kingdom for his retelling. The ending has the wicked queen don magic slippers at Snow White and the prince's wedding. The slippers force her to dance until she drops dead. Everyone else rejoices and lives happily ever after. This version is more appropriate for older children because of the amount of text, vocabulary, and mature artwork.

Rumpelstiltskin

Themes
- Greed
- Deceit
- Value of a promise
- Price of life
- Basis for marriage
- What other themes can you and your students find?

What's in a name? Names children call each other pale in comparison to these: Doppelturk, Purzinigele, Batzibitzili, Panzimanzi, Whuppity Stoorie, Ricdin-Ricdon, Titeliture, Tom-Tit-Tot, known in the U.S. and Germany as Rumpelstiltskin.

The story we know best comes from the Grimm brothers, who collected and recorded several versions during the early 1800's. They combined these versions into the one most known today. John M. Ellis, in *One Fairy Tale Too Many*, observes that the Grimms chose the most violent parts to include in their last version (79), published in English in 1823. By the time the Grimms published the story, it was well-known across Britain and Europe. The story was centuries old then, with the first print version published between 1575 and 1590 by Francois Rabelais.

The AT Index classifies "Rumpelstiltskin" as "The Name of the Helper" story, which is part of a larger group called "Spinning Women" stories. One set of these stories features three crones as helpers. The other—the Rumpelstiltskin type—features an odd male character referred to as a gnome, a dwarf, a demon, or a devil. Both crones and male characters possess supernatural talents in spinning flax or straw. The crones give a light, comic touch to the story, while the male characters cast a dark shadow. The crones only ask for kindness and acceptance in return for their labors, but the male characters demand the result of the queen's labor—her child.

The themes of this story vary greatly from those of most other tales, which promote physical beauty or virtue. "Rumpelstiltskin's" themes offer rich ground for contemplation and discussion.

Sources Consulted

Aarne, Antti. *The Types of the Folktale, a Classification and Bibliography*. Helsinki, Finland: Suomalainen Tiedeakatemia, 1961.

Ellis, John M. *One Fairy Story Too Many: The Brothers Grimm and Their Tales*. Chicago: U of Chicago P, 1983.

Heiner, Heidi Anne. "History of Rumpelstiltskin." *SurLaLune Fairy Tales*. 11 Nov. 2002. 02 June 2007 <www.surlalunefairytales.com/rumpelstiltskin/history.html>.

Opie, Iona and Peter Opie. *The Classic Fairy Tales*. New York: Oxford UP, 1974.

Zipes, Jack. *Breaking the Magic Spell: Radical Theories of Folk and Fairy Tales*. Austin: U of Texas P, 1979.

Selected Annotated Bibliography

Galdone, Paul. *Rumpelstiltskin*. Reprint ed. New York: Clarion, 1990. 32 p. Galdone's typical colorful drawings give his retelling a light-hearted tone. The story itself is based on the traditional, with Rumpelstiltskin stamping his foot and disappearing into the earth at the end.

Hamilton, Virginia. *The Girl Who Spun Gold*. Illus. Leo and Diane Dillon. New York: Blue Sky, 2000. 40 p. Hamilton bases her story on a West Indian variant of Rumpelstiltskin, Little Man, or "Lit'mahn." Its lilting language is intended to reflect the speech patterns of the West Indies. The artwork shimmers with gold. The story begins with a description of Lit'mahn and then moves to a scene where a mother tells the king that her daughter, Quashiba, can spin gold thread to make cloth for him. He marries her and tells her she has one year in which to weave him three rooms of golden things. After a year, he locks her in a room to do her weaving. Lit'mahn appears and offers his help if Quashiba will guess his name. If she can't guess, he will make her as tiny as he is and take her to live with him. He does the work, and Quashiba doesn't guess correctly until the king tells her about hearing Lit'mahn sing his name. When he hears his name, he explodes into a million flecks of gold, leaving a smell of burned feathers. Quashiba doesn't speak to the king for three years when he begs forgiveness for how he treated her. They live happily after that.

Moser, Barry. *Tucker Pfeffercorn: An Old Story Retold*. Boston: Little, 1994. n. pag. Set in mining and cotton country in the South, Tucker Pfeffercorn helps Bessie Grace spin cotton into gold for Hezakiah Sweatt, the murderous mine owner. Tucker also does away with Sweatt and helps Bessie Grace and her daughter, Claretta, escape. He comes back to claim Claretta as his prize, but allows Bessie Grace to guess his name. She happens to pass him singing a rhyme with his name in it. When she guesses correctly, he stomps until he splits himself in two.

Noël, Christopher. *Rumpelstiltskin*. Illus. Peter Sis. Edina, MN: ABDO, 2005. n. pag. Noël reinforces the German origin of this tale by using the address "Herr" and suggesting German names in the guessing game. Sis's Rumpelstiltskin appears in a red jester's suit to save the miller's daughter. His cartoonish character stands out against a more realistic background. The king is portrayed in text and art as cruel and arrogant. In this adaptation, the miller's-daughter-turned-queen herself searches for names across the country in bitter winter conditions. On her way home, she finds Rumpelstiltskin dancing by the fire and learns his name. The art and text complement each other perfectly at the end, when Rumpelstiltskin screws himself into the floor until he vanishes, leaving the queen and her child in peace.

Sage, Alison. *Rumpelstiltskin*. Illus. Gennady Spirin. New York: Dial, 1991. 30 p. Sage develops the traditional characters while following the traditional plot. In this ending, Rumpelstiltskin vanishes after stamping his foot on the floor. The tapestry-like illustrations enhance the text.

Stanley, Diane. *Rumpelstiltskin's Daughter*. Reprint ed. NY: HarperTrophy, 2002. 32 p. In this clever, humorous story, the miller's daughter and Rumpelstiltskin elope from the king's tower room filled with straw. They live happily and have a daughter. Rumpelstiltskin spins gold when they need money, which their daughter takes to town to buy supplies. The king guesses her origins and captures her to spin gold for him. Instead, she enacts a plan to cure him of his greed and ends up as prime minister.

Vande Velde, Vivian. *The Rumpelstiltskin Problem*. Boston: Houghton, 2000. 116 p. For the logic lovers among us, Vande Velde has written six short stories that address the logic problems inherent in the traditional Rumpelstiltskin story. The stories provide motivation for Rumpelstiltskin to want a baby, motivation for the miller to say that his daughter could spin straw into gold, reasons for a miller to be speaking to a king in the first place, why a being who could spin straw into gold accepts a gold ring as payment, and other answers to plot problems in the original story. Older children will enjoy the breezy tone and the more logical tales.

Zelinsky, Paul O. *Rumpelstiltskin*. Reprint ed. New York: Puffin, 1996. 40 p. Zelinsky based his Caldecott Award-winning book on the German Grimm version, with the title character riding away on a wooden cooking spoon when his name is guessed. An author note at the end gives a short history of the tale. Zelinsky's lush medieval illustrations depict the young king's riches and Rumpelstiltskin's strangeness.

Jack and the Beanstalk

Themes
- Greed
- Poverty
- Crime
- Revenge
- Curiosity
- What other themes can you and your students find?

Whether Jack is lazy, greedy, and vengeful or curious and enterprising depends on which version of "Jack and the Beanstalk" you read. The AT Index classifies this story as "The Boy Steals the Giant's Treasure" type. It identifies the three main parts of the story as expedition to the giant, giant robbed, giant captured (and often killed).

The idea of climbing to the heavens is prehistoric, dating to the Tower of Babel and Jacob's ladder. Norse mythology's Yggdrasill, an ash tree, bridges heaven and earth. Asians have a similar story about a branch of Buddha's tree. The Grimms recorded a similar story in Germany using turnip seeds, rather than Jack's beans. Versions of the story are well known in Britain, Western Europe, French-speaking Canada, and Canadian Native American tribes.

The first printed version of "Jack and the Beanstalk" was a British skit script published in 1734. The skit seems to have been produced and published to poke fun at the type of person who would enjoy such a story, showing it as nonsense.

Nowadays, two British versions provide the basis for most versions since, with neither version considered definitive. Benjamin Tabart's version was printed in 1807.

The Tabart version won out over another version also published in 1807 by B.A.T., *The History of Mother Twaddle, and the Marvellous Atchievements of Her Son Jack*. This story differed significantly from Tabart's and has not influenced other, later versions.

Several major details differentiate Tabart from the other well-known one by Joseph Jacob published in 1890. In Tabart, Jack is lazy and treats his mother poorly. He acts under orders from a fairy at the top of the beanstalk. She tells him to steal from and kill the giant because the giant once stole from and killed Jack's father. Jack consults his mother before climbing the beanstalk and thinks things through each time. Jack obeys the fairy and gets revenge. In the end, Jack promises to be a better person and lives with his mother happily ever after. In this version, the giant says, "I smell fresh meat."

In Jacob's version, Jack and his mother suffer from extreme poverty. Jack acts of his own accord, not on the command of a fairy. When the beanstalk grows, Jack climbs it in curiosity and steals the giant's treasures. He and his mother live well on the bag of gold, but when it runs out, he goes back up the beanstalk for more. After stealing the hen that laid golden eggs, they are set for life, but Jack wants even more and goes back for the golden harp. In the end, Jack marries a princess, and they and his mother live together happily ever after. In this version, the giant says, "Fee-fi-fo-fum."

Themes vary, too, depending on the version, but in each case, Jack's behavior rewards him and his mother.

Sources Consulted

Aarne, Antti. *The Types of the Folktale, a Classification and Bibliography*. Helsinki, Finland: Suomalainen Tiedeakatemia, 1961.

Bettelheim, Bruno. *Uses of Enchantment*. New York: Knopf, 1977.

Heiner, Heidi Anne. "History of Jack and the Beanstalk." *SurLaLune Fairy Tales*. 18 Dec. 2003. 02 June 2007
<www.surlalunefairytales.com/jackbeanstalk/history.html>.

Opie, Iona and Peter Opie. *The Classic Fairy Tales*. New York: Oxford UP, 1974.

Selected Annotated Bibliography

Baca, Ana. *Chiles for Benito/Chiles para Benito*. Illus. Anthony Accardo. Houston: Piñata, 2002. 28 p. This English and Spanish version of a New Mexican tale has Benito sell his cow to get magic chili seeds from a man with a talking bird. He plants them, and they grow like weeds. Not knowing what they are, Benito's neighbors complain that the weeds will take over their fields. Benito works hard to chop the plants down, but they come right back. Then he notices strange red fruit. He likes the sweet, hot taste, and shows his mother. The man who sold him the seeds returns, but this time his bird is silent and the man talks. He gives Benito, his mother, and the neighbors recipes for chilies. The people have grown and eaten chilies ever since. The book contains a recipe for red chili sauce.

Beneduce, Ann Keay. *Jack and the Beanstalk*. Illus. Gennady Spirin. New York: Philomel, 1999. 32 p. Jack and his mother live outside London. Jack's main trait, curiosity, gets him into predicaments. He is curious about the ten magic beans for which he traded the cow. His curiosity leads him to climb the beanstalk that grows from the beans when his mother throws them out the window. He is curious about the beautiful woman he meets at the top of the beanstalk. She turns out to be his father's fairy guardian. She tells him that the giant killed his father, and he must avenge his father. Jack's curiosity leads him to the giant's castle, where a motherly woman warns him about the giant, but takes him in. Jack is clever as well as curious and uses his wits to retrieve his father's fortune, the hen that lays golden eggs, and magic harp. Jack beats the giant down the beanstalk and chops the stalk down. The giant falls to his death. Watercolor and tempera illustrations depict medieval settings and intricate page borders. An author note gives a brief history of the tale.

Birdseye, Tom. *Look Out, Jack! The Giant Is Back!* Illus. Will Hillenbrand. New York: Holiday House, 2001. 32 p. This story picks up where "Jack and the Beanstalk" left off. Instead of the projected "happily ever after," the dead giant's brother appears, and he is even nastier than the deceased. He wants revenge on Jack, so Jack packs up his mother and things and takes a boat to America. There he raises roses on a farm in North Carolina. The giant finds Jack and demands his brother's loot back. Jack and his mother cook a Southern picnic feast that Jack loads along with the loot onto his mules and takes it up the mountain. The giant is annoyed that Jack isn't scared. Jack offers his picnic, and the angry giant eats it all. The giant demands the loot, but is too full of food to catch Jack as he runs away. The giant ends up stomping so hard that the mountain falls in on top of him, and Jack and his mama enjoy farm life, roses, and the loot. The light-hearted illustrations add to the fun. One double spread is arranged vertically to take in the giant's size.

DeSpain, Pleasant. *Strongheart Jack and the Beanstalk*. Illus. Joe Shlichta. Little Rock, AR: August, 1997. 32 p. The author's opening note gives a short history of the tale and offers suggestions on how to present the story. DeSpain's version, based on the earliest versions, paints Jack as lazy. He trades the cow for magic beans, which enrages his mother, who throws the beans out the window. Overnight, the beanstalk grows. Jack's mother gives him her husband's sword to help him on his journey up the beanstalk with his cat, Octavia. Octavia helps Jack overcome his first test, passing the cactus guards. Then Octavia fills Jack in on the mystery surrounding Jack's father—he was killed and eaten by a giant to whom he had been kind. Jack realizes he's never really been lazy, just without purpose, and now revenge becomes his purpose. A yellow tortoise offers a riddle and advice to keep one's heart strong. They enter the castle, and are assisted by Elinor, a maiden the giant captured. Jack steals the dungeon key from around the giant's neck and gives it to Elinor, who sets out to free her captive brother. He gets free, but Elinor falls dead when she steps outside because, unbeknown to her, she is cursed. Jack, Octavia, and the giant battle. Jack and Octavia run to the beanstalk with the giant close behind. Jack hacks the beanstalk with his sword. The giant falls to the ground, dead. His death releases enchantments, bringing Elinor alive to Jack via the Fairy Harp. They marry and live happily ever after.

Haley, Gail E. *Jack and the Bean Tree*. New York: Knopf, 1986. 48 p. Set in Appalachia, the narrator is Poppyseed, a storytellin' woman who has many Jack stories. She narrates in dialect, which may be challenging for younger readers. Poverty-stricken, Jack's maw orders him to sell the cow. He trades the cow for three magic beans, to his mother's distress. The beans grow overnight and Jack "clomb and clomb" to the top where he meets the giant's wife, Matilda, and then the unfriendly giant, Ephidophilus. Jack steals the giant's magic cloth and takes it home, where it feeds him and his maw and cleans up. Curiosity makes Jack go back up the beanstalk. This time Jack steals the hen that lays golden eggs. He goes up the beanstalk once more and steals the magic harp with Ephidophilus hot on his heels. Jack makes it back and cuts the beanstalk down with his axe. The fall kills the giant, and Jack and his mother get along fine after that. The illustrations clearly evoke mountain life and a fearsome giant and his habitat.

Harris, Jim. *Jack and the Giant: A Story Full of Beans*. Flagstaff, AZ: Rising Moon, 1997. 32 p. Harris's humorous illustrations add to the fun of this Jack story set in the old West. Jack trades his milk cow, Fred, for a hand full of beans and some used chewing gum, infuriating his mother. The beans grow a huge stalk overnight, which Jack climbs to find his cow and an adobe castle. The resident giant turns out to be Wild Bill Hiccup, the cattle rustler. He has a magic lasso and magic buffalo that make gold. Jack confronts Wild Bill, grabs the giant's banjo and lasso, and gallops out the door on the magic buffalo. Jack snaps the giant off the beanstalk. The giant's landing creates the Grand Canyon. Jack's ma is happy with his loot, which makes their ranch the biggest spread west of the Mississippi.

Lorenz, Albert. *Jack and the Beanstalk*. Abrams, 2002. 40 p. Lorenz's detailed illustrations include several challenges to find Jack. The castle, decorated with gold skulls and guarded by vultures, looks forbidding. Keeping Jack small in scale with the giant and his surroundings helps readers put themselves in Jack's place. Though small, Jack uses creative means to best the giant, as he steals gold on one trip, the hen that lays golden eggs on another trip, and the golden harp on another trip. On the last trip, the giant and his wife come after him, but Jack and his mother chop down the beanstalk in time. The giant and his wife fall into the sea, never to be seen again. Jack and his mother share their wealth with the town, and they all live happily ever after. An author's note at the end explains the concept of scale and the themes the author-illustrator is trying to convey.

Osborne, Mary Pope. *Kate and the Beanstalk*. Illus. Giselle Potter. New York: Atheneum, 2000. 40 p. Unlike the usual lazy Jack, the star of this story, Kate, loves to help. She is happy to take the cow to market. However, she falls prey to the same foolishness as the usual Jack, trading the cow for magic beans. Kate watches the beanstalk grow in the middle of the night and begins climbing until she reaches the castle at the top. She meets a woman who gives her background about the giant killing the noble knight who owned the castle. His wife and child were visiting "below," and stayed there for safety, but are now in poverty. Kate admits to fearing nothing when she's doing right. The woman sends Kate on a quest for a hen that lays golden eggs, a bag filled with gold coins, and a magic harp. If Kate finds and returns these to the knight's widow, they won't starve. Kate accepts the challenge and is soon picked up by the giant's wife to help her cook. She steals the hen, takes it home, and hides it. Then she disguises herself and goes back up. The giant's wife picks her up to help serve. Kate steals the money bag, takes it home, and hides it. She disguises herself once more and goes up the beanstalk where she is picked up by the giant's wife to be a servant. Kate snatches the magic harp and climbs down the beanstalk, with the giant close at her heels. She chops the stalk with an axe, bringing down the giant, who dies in the fall. Kate's mother recognizes him as the giant who killed her husband, and Kate learns her true identity. Kate, her mother, and the Queen of the Fairies take a chariot up to their castle where they employ the giant's wife as their cook.

Strickland, Brad and Thomas E. Fuller. *Jack and the Beanstalk*. Allen, TX: Little Red Chair, 1999. 94 p. The first of the Wishbone, the Early Years series designed for second graders and up, retells the classic tale with Wishbone, the Jack Russell terrier, as the hero. The story alternates between a contemporary school story featuring third graders and Jack and the Beanstalk. Jack's father has been killed by a giant who stole his treasures, a goose that lays golden eggs, a magic harp, and a magic axe. Facing starvation, Wishbone, as Jack, takes the cow to be sold. On the way, he meets a stranger who trades him three magic beans for the cow. The beanstalk grows, and Jack climbs it to see what's at the top. The Good Fairy challenges Jack's bravery and urges him to retrieve his father's treasures from the giant's castle. He meets a servant girl who wants to be rescued. She helps Jack get the golden goose, magic harp, and magic axe before the giant starts chasing them. With the giant hot on their heels, Jack heads down the beanstalk with the Good Fairy assuring him he'll know what to do. When he and his treasures return home, he calls the axe into action to chop the beanstalk. There is no sign of the giant, only a huge crater where he fell. In the contemporary story, Joe takes Wishbone to school for show and tell. Wishbone leaves his favorite ball at school and wants it back. He runs away from Joe and sneaks into the school when the custodian props the door open but is caught in a classroom before he finds his ball. The custodian calls Joe's house. Joe and his mom come to get Wishbone, and Joe is in trouble for not watching Wishbone better. Wishbone wiggles free one more time and dashes into the correct classroom to find his ball. They all lived happily ever after. A brief history of "Jack and the Beanstalk" ends the book.

Walker, Richard. *Jack and the Beanstalk*. Illus. Niamh Sharkey. New York: Barefoot, 1999. 32 p. In this retelling, both Jack and his mother are lazy about doing work. When they run out of food and money, Jack takes the cow to market to sell. He trades it for six magic beans instead. Jack's mother throws the beans out the window where they grow into a tall stalk in the middle of the night. Jack climbs it to see where it goes. Jack reaches the giant's castle, where a woman takes him in, but warns him about the giant. Jack steals a bag of gold and takes it home. He immediately goes back for more. The goose that laid the golden egg asks Jack if it can go home with him. Then the woman asks if she can come with him. Jack agrees and goes back for the magic harp when the giant awakens and chases Jack. Jack and his entourage slither down the stalk with the giant close behind. Jack, the woman, the goose, and the harp make it safely home. The giant is on top of the beanstalk, so Jack bends it down as far as he can and lets it go, catapulting the giant into space. Funny illustrations give Jack an elfin air.

Hansel and Gretel

> **Themes**
> - Abandonment
> - Independence
> - Teamwork
> - Poverty
> - Trust
> - Survival in nature
> - What other themes can you and your students find?

Hansel and Gretel are known as two abandoned children who use their strength and wits to save their lives. The 1853 English version of the Grimm tale finds roots in several earlier stories. The AT Index classifies "Hansel and Gretel" as one of the "Children and the Ogre" stories. "Jack and the Beanstalk" is sometimes connected to this type, too, as both stories share young characters defeating supernatural beings.

"The Children and the Ogre" type was well known in Europe, especially in the Baltic countries (Opie 308). France's Perrault and Madame d'Alnoy published stories in 1697 and 1721, respectively, which may have influenced the Grimms' 1853 version. An earlier Swedish tale tells of a captured boy holding out a stick instead of his finger, similar to Hansel's action, when asked if he were fat enough. The gingerbread house has a precedent in an early fourteenth-century Spanish manuscript describing an abbey made of food (Opie 310).

Sources interested in an historical perspective remind us that because of extreme poverty among the working class of Europe's feudal system, parents could have actually abandoned their children to save themselves. Stepmothers were also common due to mothers dying in childbirth or from disease (Zipes, *Breaking* 32; Tatar, 49-50).

Zipes (*Breaking* 32) says that the witch symbolizes the feudal aristocracy, ready to gobble up anyone smaller than they are. Lüthi, however, maintains that the witch represents evil and ironically dies of methods she made herself (*Once* 64).

Like "Jack and the Beanstalk," "Hansel and Gretel" begins in the reality of poverty. Unlike Jack's going after the giant, Hansel and Gretel did not deliberately seek the witch. Hansel and Gretel exert individual power by inventing their own clever ways of surviving in the woods and defeating the witch. They do it without the usual fairy tale magic, except for a few birds that give directions and a duck that paddles them across a lake toward home.

Though the premise is disturbing and touches upon one of children's greatest fears, abandonment, Hansel and Gretel's triumph can empower readers.

Sources Consulted

Aarne, Antti. *The Types of the Folktale, a Classification and Bibliography*. Helsinki, Finland: Suomalainen Tiedeakatemia, 1961.

Bettelheim, Bruno. *Uses of Enchantment*. New York: Knopf, 1977.

Heiner, Heidi Anne. "History of Hansel and Gretel." *SurLaLune Fairy Tales*. 1 Dec. 2002. 02 June 2007 <www.surlalunefairytales.com/hanselgretel/history.html>.

Lüthi, Max. *Once Upon a Time: On the Nature of Fairy Tales*. Bloomington: Indiana UP, 1970.

Opie, Iona and Peter Opie. *The Classic Fairy Tales*. New York: Oxford UP, 1974.

Tatar, Maria. *The Hard Facts of the Grimms' Fairy Tales*. Princeton, N.J.: Princeton UP, 1987.

Zipes, Jack. *Breaking the Magic Spell: Radical Theories of Folk and Fairy Tales*. Austin: U of Texas P, 1979.

Selected Annotated Bibliography

Grimm, Jacob and Wilhelm Grimm. *Hansel and Gretel*. Trans. Anthea Bell. Illus. Dorothée Duntze. New York: North-South, 2001. 32 p. Originally published in Switzerland, this translation's artwork reflects Western European life long ago and modern Western European art. Hansel and Gretel in traditional costume wander through an abstract forest of grays, blues, and browns. The gingerbread house is pure delight, except for the witch peeking out the window. This translation keeps the Grimms' references to God in a few places.

Jeffers, Susan. *Hansel and Gretel*. Reprint ed. New York: Puffin, 1993. 32 p. Jeffers's drawings contrast the children's innocence with the beautiful, benign, natural world and the witch's evil in this traditional story. This version includes a white bird leading them to the gingerbread house, Gretel shoving the witch into the oven, and a little duck to carry them across the lake.

North, Carol. *Hansel and Gretel*. Illus. Terri Super. New York: Golden, 1990. 24 p. This is a short, appropriate version for young children. Text and illustrations are friendly and accessible. Hansel and Gretel conquer the witch and run home with their pockets full of jewels, meeting their father on the way, as he is out looking for them.

Ray, Jane. *Hansel and Gretel*. Cambridge, MA: Candlewick, 1997. n. pag. Ray's folk-art style illustrations bring a soulful quality to her retelling, capturing the children's fear, confusion, and love for each other. The emotional impact of the artwork makes this version more appropriate for older children. The text is true to the traditional tale.

Sathre, Vivian. *Hansel and Gretel*. Allen, TX: Little Red Chair, 1999. 93 p. Number 3 in the Wishbone, the Early Years series alternates a contemporary school story with "Hansel and Gretel." Wishbone, the Jack Russell terrier, is the hero of both, at least in his own mind. The Early Years series is written for third graders.

Wallace, Ian. *Hansel and Gretel*. Toronto: Groundwood, 1996. 32 p. The pastel illustrations on black paper by Canadian artist Wallace give this adaptation a dark feel. Though most of the story is traditional, the father is a fisherman, and the family lives on the Atlantic's north coast. Because the final illustration seems to indicate lurking evil, this story may not be appropriate for younger students.

Section II

The Lessons

Reading

Fairy Tale Dictionary

Supports AASL standards   1, 5, 6
Supports NCTE standards   1, 2, 3, 6, 8, 9, 12

This lesson develops comprehension and context skills. Fairy tales and their many versions contain uncommon words. To extend students' vocabulary, encourage proper language usage, and reinforce dictionary skills, have them each make fairy tale dictionaries. Give each student a small notebook or fold several plain 8.5 x 11 inch sheets of paper in half and staple them on the side to create a 5.5 x 8.5 inch booklet. Encourage students to decorate the covers and write their names on them. Adding alphabet tabs to every two or three pages is optional, but helpful. If you do not add tabs, have students write letter headings at the top of the pages.

Tell students that as they read fairy tales, they will probably see words they don't know. Have them write down those words in their dictionary on the proper alphabet page. Ask them to guess the meaning based on context and then look the word up in a dictionary. Their own entries should include the following:

- The unfamiliar word
- The country or language where the word originated (optional)
- The part of speech, if students have learned them
- The definition
- The pronunciation (have students write the word phonetically)
- The sentence in which the word was used in the fairy tale

> ### ✱ Alternate Activity
>
> Instead of a printed version, students can
>
> - Create their individual dictionaries in a computer word processing file
> - Contribute to a classroom dictionary in a computer word processing file
> - Create and develop a word wall, with words written on large pieces of paper and affixed to a designated wall or bulletin board
> - Make a set of flash cards, with an illustration on one side and the vocabulary word on the other

Repeat After Me

Supports AASL standards   1, 2, 3, 5, 6, 9
Supports NCTE standards   1, 3, 6, 11

This lesson helps students recognize patterns, understand story structure, and practice predicting within a fairy tale. Before you read a fairy tale aloud, ask students to listen for repeated words, phrases, and ideas. Tell students to write them down to discuss later. Read the tale. Then ask students for repetitions. Ask why they think the author included them. Answers include helping listeners remember, reinforcing important details, adding rhythm to the story (in the case of a refrain, such as "Fee, fi, fo, fum"), and giving the story unity.

"Unity" refers to the parts of the story working together to create a satisfying whole. Repetition creates boundaries in which the author creates a world and the listener hears it. Finally, ask students if they thought the repetitions were effective. If so, how? If not, what would they have done differently?

Commonalities

Supports AASL standards   1, 2, 3, 6, 7, 9
Supports NCTE standards   1, 3, 6, 10, 11

This lesson will reinforce story structure and pattern recognition skills, giving students practice in seeing patterns among different stories. Ask students to read three or more different fairy tales (not different versions of the same tale). If your class has students whose first language is not English, allow them to read fairy tales in their own languages or from their own cultures. Tell them to watch for things in the stories that are similar. Distribute the "Commonalities Template," Figure 1.1 for students to complete, either individually or in small groups. Then discuss the results.

Commonalities

Name _____ Date _____

Titles of fairy tales I read

1. _____
    author (if there is one) _____
2. _____
    author (if there is one) _____
3. _____
    author (if there is one) _____

I noticed that the stories' characters are alike in these ways:
_____
_____
_____

The story beginnings are alike in these ways:
_____
_____
_____

The story endings are alike in these ways:
_____
_____
_____

The action in the stories was alike in these ways:
_____
_____
_____

Here are other things I thought were alike:
_____
_____
_____

Figure 1.1: Commonalities Template

From *Once Upon A Time: Fairy Tales in the Library and Language Arts Classroom for Grades 3-6*, by Jane Heitman. Columbus, OH: Linworth Publishing, Inc. Further reproduction prohibited. Copyright ©2007.

> **Extended Activity**
>
> Use the results to write your own classroom definition of fairy tales. Use information from "Section I, What Is a Fairy Tale?" in this book or other resources to enrich students' understanding.

Story Element Study

Plot

Map That Plot

Supports AASL standards   1, 2, 3, 4, 9
Supports NCTE standards   1, 3, 6, 11, 12

This lesson will especially appeal to your visual learners and will help the whole class see story structure, which will aid comprehension. Define "plot" as "the action of the story" or "what happens in the story." Stories typically contain a beginning, middle, and end. The twists, turns, hills, and valleys along the way make one plot different from another.

Tell the class to pay close attention to the action of the fairy tale you are going to read to them. Have them listen for parts that are slow, fast, exciting, and less exciting. Then read a fairy tale aloud.

Use a white board, projected overhead transparency, or other medium so all students can see. Then map the story together. Begin low and flat, allowing for the action to rise as the plot gets more exciting. Ask the students to tell you how high and in what order each story action should go. As you draw your map, jot down keywords indicating what happened at that spot.

If appropriate for your students' abilities, define and identify the following plot-related terms.

> **Introduction:** The beginning. Indicates setting and characters, and hints at problems that are a basis for plot.
>
> **Rising action:** What happens. The longest part of the story where the problems become more and more difficult.
>
> **Climax:** The high point or turning point of a story. Often one extreme action or definite decision.
>
> **Falling action:** What happens to wrap up the story
>
> **Conclusion:** Usually very short statement or paragraph to sum up. In fairy tales, usually "They lived happily ever after."

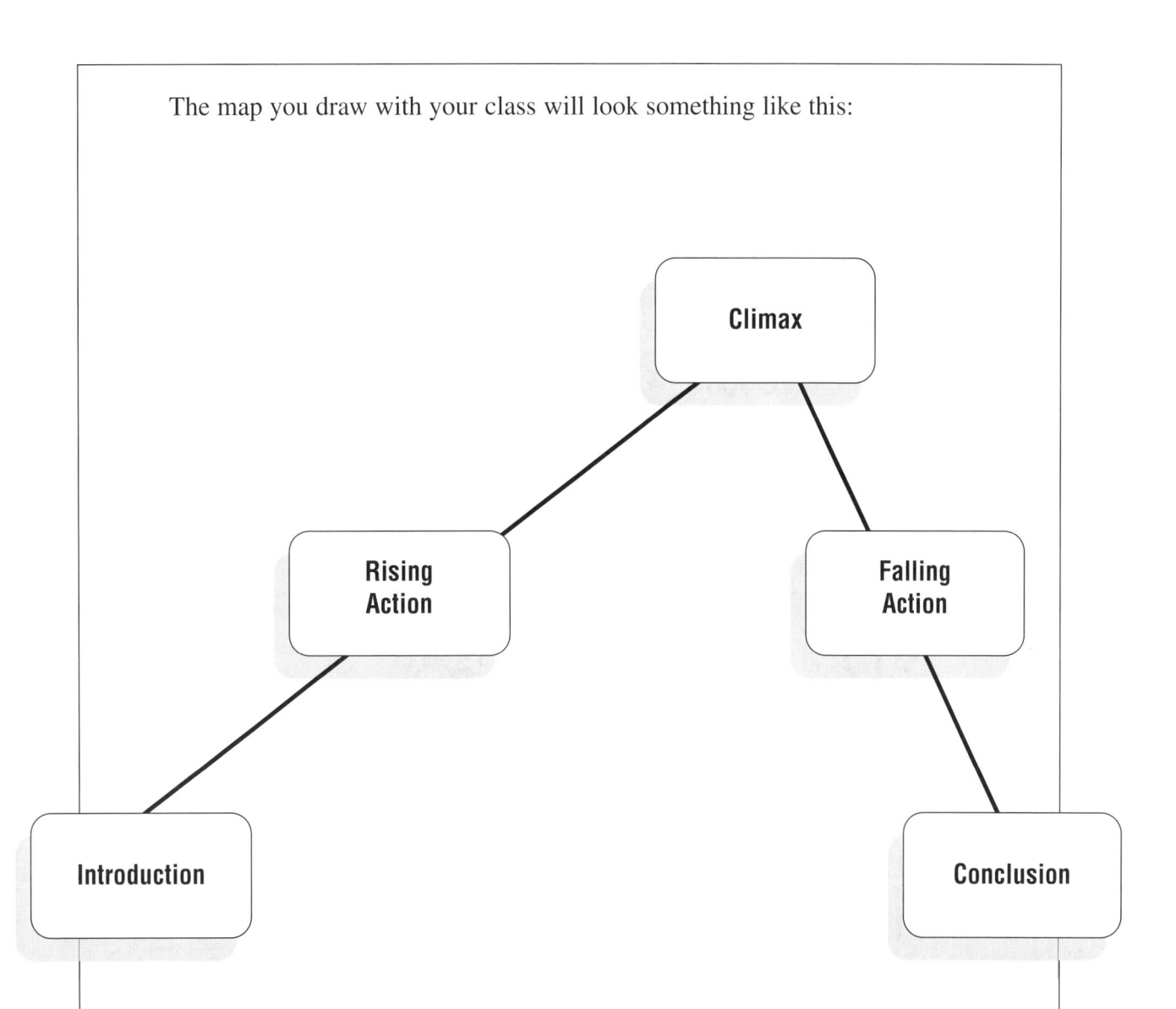

The map you draw with your class will look something like this:

```
                        Climax
                       /      \
                      /        \
                Rising          Falling
                Action          Action
               /                      \
              /                        \
        Introduction                 Conclusion
```

When students understand the concepts, ask them to work with a partner or in groups. Distribute Figure 1.3, Story Map Template to each group. They will read a fairy tale and make their own story map, presenting it to the class when they are finished. Display the completed maps and discuss the differences and similarities.

Figure 1.2: Story Map Example

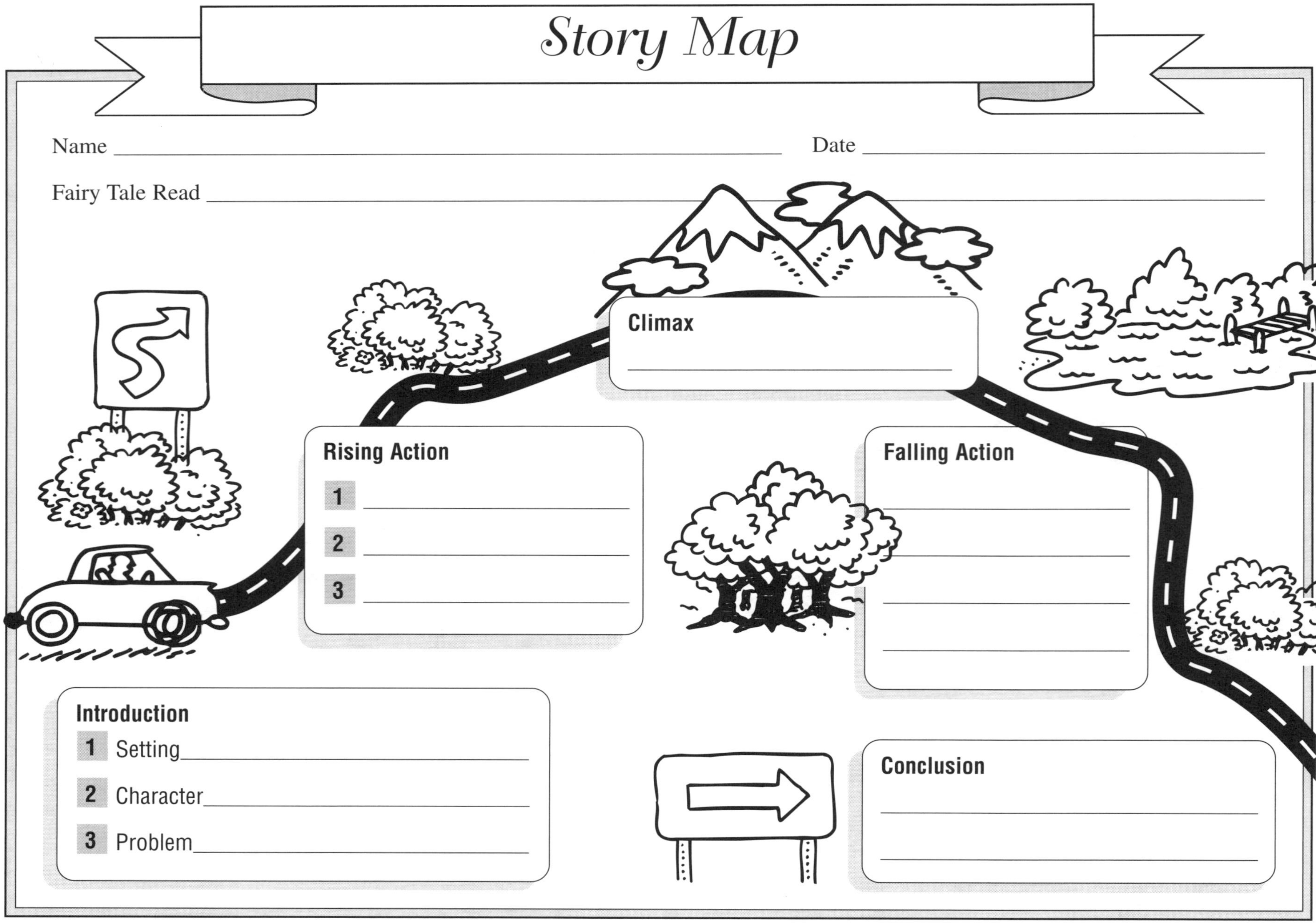

Story Map

Name _____ Date _____

Fairy Tale Read _____

Climax

Falling Action

Rising Action
1 _____
2 _____
3 _____

Introduction
1 Setting _____
2 Character _____
3 Problem _____

Conclusion

Figure 1.3: Story Map Template

From *Once Upon A Time: Fairy Tales in the Library and Language Arts Classroom for Grades 3-6*, by Jane Heitman. Columbus, OH: Linworth Publishing, Inc. Further reproduction prohibited. Copyright ©2007

Putting It Together

Supports AASL standards   1, 2, 3, 5, 6, 9
Supports NCTE standards   1, 3, 6, 11

This lesson develops students' sequencing and critical thinking skills. Choose a fairy tale and type it, taking care to comply with copyright laws. Leave breaks after every three or four sentences. Then print the tale. Students will work in groups of four or five, so make as many copies as you will need for the class. Cut the tale apart where the breaks are and put the pieces for each tale in an envelope.

Give one envelope to each group of four or five students. Tell them they have all the pieces to a fairy tale, but they must put the story in the correct order. When they are ready, they will read their story to the class.

Working in groups or with partners enables special learners and English language learners to participate without being singled out. Groups may need to be reminded to allow all members to contribute and to help teach each other.

* Alternate Activity

- Prepare several different stories in the way described previously, so that student groups are each working on a different story.
- The library media specialist will create a Fairy Tale Learning Center in the library. Have one or more stories prepared in envelopes as described previously along with books containing the tales. Allow individual students to put the story pieces in order. They can check their own work by finding and reading the tale from the book.

Four Main Things Sandwich

Supports AASL standards   1, 2, 3, 5, 6, 9
Supports NCTE standards   1, 3, 6, 11

This simple lesson helps students demonstrate comprehension and identify the main action of the story. Before you read a fairy tale aloud, ask your students to listen for the four main things that happen between "Once upon a time" and "They lived happily ever after" (or whatever the opening and closing lines are of the story you chose). Read the story. Then tell the students that listing the four main things in the plot is like putting together a sandwich. The bottom piece of bread is the introduction. The top piece of bread is the conclusion. The real meat or filling is the action.

Distribute Figure 1.4, the Four Main Things Sandwich sheet, and complete it together as a class, based on the fairy tale you read.

Then distribute another Four Main Things Sandwich sheet. Ask students to read a fairy tale on their own and complete the sheet. Allow special learners or English language learners to draw the four main scenes or use keywords to indicate the main action. Let students share their results in small groups or with the entire class. If several students choose the same tale, see how similar or different they are.

▶ Extended Activity

After students have chosen their sandwich "fillings," have them add special sauces, pickles, and spices to represent minor action.

Confounded Conflict

Supports AASL standards   1, 2, 3, 5, 6, 9
Supports NCTE standards   1, 3, 6, 11

Cause and effect, critical thinking, and comprehension are the focus of this lesson. The middle of a story contains most of the plot's action, following the problem introduced in the beginning. Characters meet obstacles preventing them from getting what they want. Usually, each obstacle is more difficult than the last. Problems and obstacles are called "conflict" in the story.

Types of Conflict

The main character's problem is with:

- Another character: Character against character
- Something in the natural world: Character against nature
- His or her conscience: Character against self
- A societal institution or code of behavior: Character against society

Read one or two fairy tales aloud or refer to tales students know. Ask them to identify the main type of conflict. Distribute Figure 1.5, Confounded Conflict Worksheet to all students. Then have the students read three fairy tale versions on their own. They will report the main types of conflict they found to the class.

Four Main Things Sandwich

Name _____ Date _____

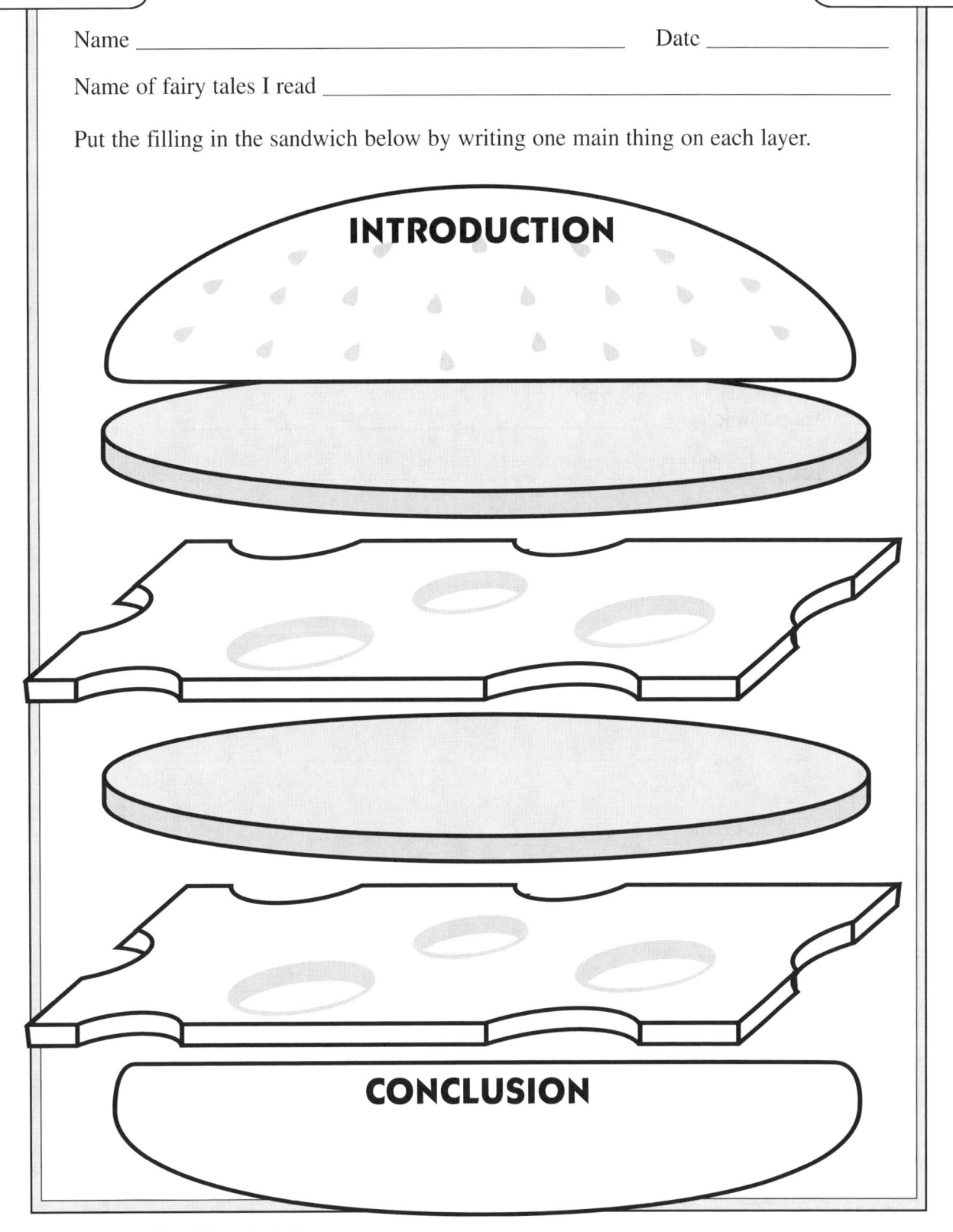

Name of fairy tales I read _____

Put the filling in the sandwich below by writing one main thing on each layer.

INTRODUCTION

CONCLUSION

Figure 1.4: Four Main Things Sandwich

From *Once Upon A Time: Fairy Tales in the Library and Language Arts Classroom for Grades 3-6*, by Jane Heitman. Columbus, OH: Linworth Publishing, Inc. Further reproduction prohibited. Copyright ©2007.

Confounded Conflict Worksheet

Name _____ Date _____

Read three fairy tales. Write the correct type of main conflict for each and give an example from the story.

Types of conflict are Character against Character, Character against Nature, Character against Him or Herself, Character against Society.

1. Fairy Tale Title _____

   Author (if one is given) _____

   Type of conflict _____

   An example is _____

   _____

2. Fairy Tale Title _____

   Author (if one is given) _____

   Type of conflict _____

   An example is _____

   _____

3. Fairy Tale Title _____

   Author (if one is given) _____

   Type of conflict _____

   An example is _____

   _____

Figure 1.5: Confounded Conflict Worksheet

From *Once Upon A Time: Fairy Tales in the Library and Language Arts Classroom for Grades 3-6*, by Jane Heitman. Columbus, OH: Linworth Publishing, Inc. Further reproduction prohibited. Copyright ©2007.

Types of Conflict

Plot Ping-Pong

Supports AASL standards 1, 2, 3, 5, 6, 9
Supports NCTE standards 1, 3, 6, 11

This lesson helps students understand cause and effect and develops their comprehension and critical thinking skills.

In most story plots, as in life, one action causes another action to happen. Read aloud to students a fairy tale all the way through. Then tell students that you will read the story again, but this time you will stop when the main character makes a major action or decision. Students will call out the result, or effect, of this action or decision. If the response is not truly cause and effect, point out faulty logic and ask students to try again. When students are correct, continue reading until you get to the next major action or decision. Continue in this manner to the end of the story.

Next, have each student work with a partner. Distribute to each pair, Figure 1.6, Plot Ping-Pong worksheets. Together, they will read a fairy tale. They will identify a major action or decision and write it on one side. Then they will decide what the effect of the action or decision is and write it on the other side. When they are finished, they should read their worksheet to the class or small group in ping-pong style, with one partner reading the cause, and the other reading the effect. Students who are listening should be alert for any problems in logic.

Once Upon a Beginning

Supports AASL standards 1, 2, 3, 5, 6, 9
Supports NCTE standards 1, 3, 6, 11, 12

This lesson teaches students what a good story beginning should include, focusing on comprehension, critical thinking, and story structure. Ask students how most fairy tales begin, and they will say, "Once upon a time." Tell students that story beginnings (the first paragraph or page) usually introduce the following:

- The main character
- Where the story happens
- When the story happens
- The main character's problem that will move the plot

Read aloud the first paragraph of several fairy tales and have students identify which of the above elements are included. Distribute Figure 1.7, Once Upon a Beginning worksheet. Then have the students read, alone or with a partner, the beginnings of three fairy tale versions. They will write the typical beginning elements found in each. Next, they will decide which beginning is the best and why. When they are finished, they will share their results with partners or small groups.

Plot Ping-Pong

Name _____ Date _____

Fairy Tale Title _____

On the left side of the ping-pong net, write a major action or decision (cause). On the right side of the ping-pong net, write the result of the action or decision (effect). Use another sheet if you need more space.

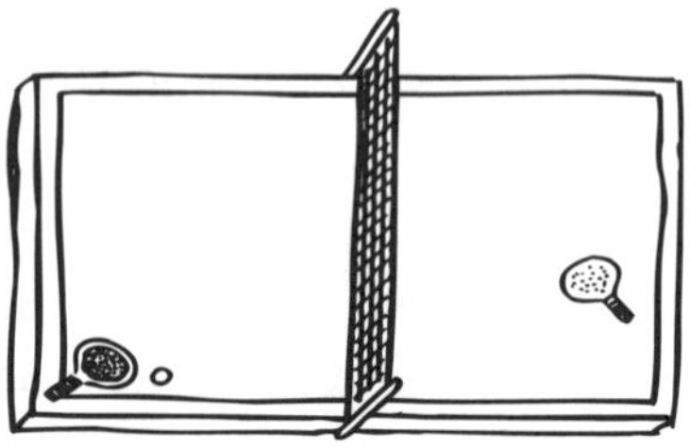

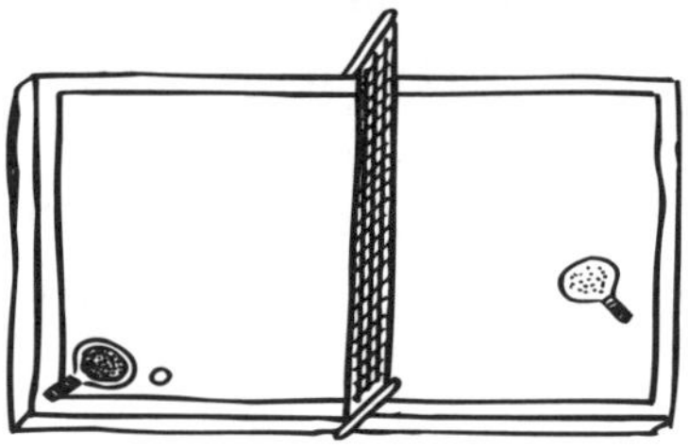

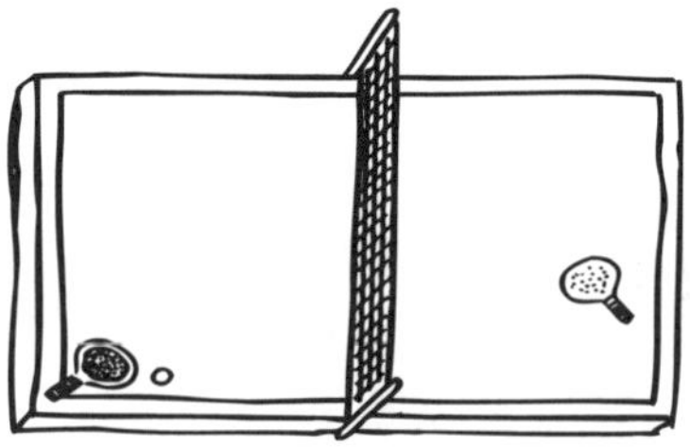

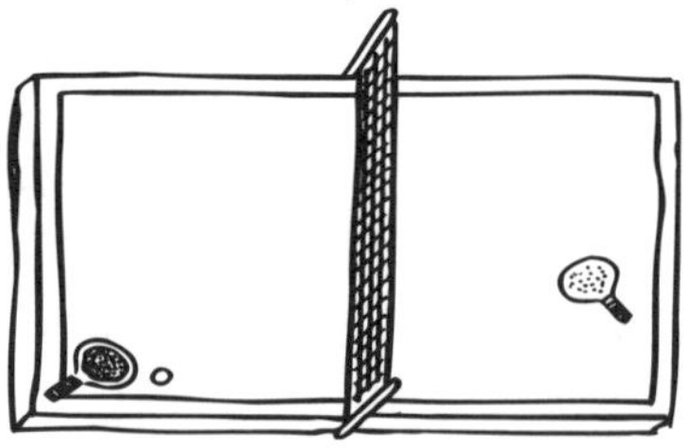

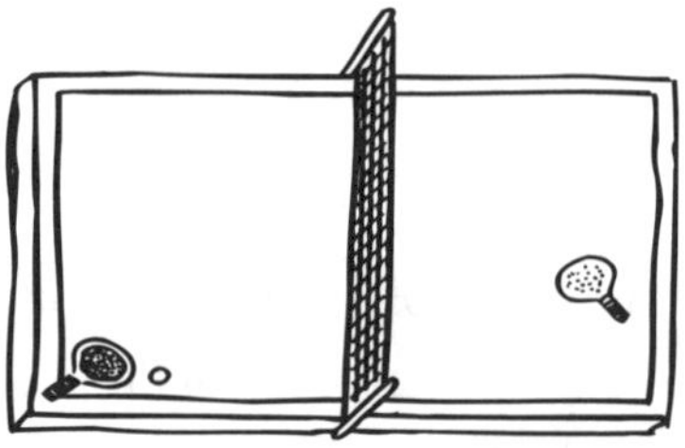

Figure 1.6: Plot Ping-Pong

From *Once Upon A Time: Fairy Tales in the Library and Language Arts Classroom for Grades 3-6*, by Jane Heitman. Columbus, OH: Linworth Publishing, Inc. Further reproduction prohibited. Copyright ©2007.

Once Upon A Beginning

Name _____ Date _____

Read the first paragraph of three versions of fairy tales and complete the blanks below.

1. Title _____

   Author (if there is one) _____

   Main character _____

   Where the story happens _____

   When the story happens _____

   Problem _____

1. Title _____

   Author (if there is one) _____

   Main character _____

   Where the story happens _____

   When the story happens _____

   Problem _____

3. Title _____

   Author (if there is one) _____

   Main character _____

   Where the story happens _____

   When the story happens _____

   Problem _____

   I think the best beginning is number _____ because _____

Figure 1.7: Once Upon A Beginning

From *Once Upon A Time: Fairy Tales in the Library and Language Arts Classroom for Grades 3-6*, by Jane Heitman. Columbus, OH: Linworth Publishing, Inc. Further reproduction prohibited. Copyright ©2007.

Resolved!

Supports AASL standards   1, 2, 3, 5, 6, 9
Supports NCTE standards   1, 3, 6, 11

This lesson will teach students the aspects of plot resolution beyond "happily ever after." Students will demonstrate comprehension and critical thinking, and learn about story structure. Explain to students that a good story ending (the last paragraph or page) wraps up the plot in a satisfying way, logically and completely. Each of the main characters should be accounted for. The main characters' problems are usually resolved in their favor, with hints of the outcome sprinkled throughout the plot. If the main characters' problems are not resolved in their favor, the reason must be clear and believable, also hinted at throughout the plot.

Read aloud one or two endings of fairy tales with which students are familiar. If they have not heard the tale for a while, read the whole story, and then re-read the ending. Discuss how satisfying the ending is based on what they expected to happen. Ask if all the characters' actions have been resolved. Is the main character's problem solved in a logical way? How would they improve the ending?

Distribute Figure 1.8, Resolved! Worksheet. Students will read a fairy tale, study the ending, and complete the worksheet. When they are done, they will report their findings in small groups or to the whole class.

And Then What Happened?

Supports AASL standards   2, 3, 5, 6, 9
Supports NCTE standards   1, 3, 11, 12

This lesson helps students hone inference, critical thinking, and predicting skills. Assign all students to read the same fairy tale or read a fairy tale to them. When finished, ask students, "And then what happened?" Have them account for the futures of all major characters. Discuss possibilities as a class or in small groups that report to the class. Help students decide why some suggestions are more likely than others.

✻ Alternate Activity

Allow students to read a fairy tale of their own choosing and answer the question, "And then what happened?", reporting to their small group or to the class. They may tell it as a report or story or they may act it out as a drama or puppet show.

Resolved! Worksheet

Name _____ Date _____

Read a fairy tale. Then complete the worksheet below about the tale's ending.

Fairy Tale Title _____

Author (if one is given) _____

Name of main character _____

    Problem solved in his or her favor? _____

Name of other character _____

    What happens to him or her?_____

Name of other character _____

What happens to him or her?_____

Name of other character _____

    What happens to him or her?_____

Name of other character _____

    What happens to him or her?_____

(Add more on your own paper if you need to.)

    Did the ending make sense? _____

    What were some clues from the story that predicted the ending?_____

    _____

    How would you have written the ending differently? _____

    _____

    What clues from the story would make your ending logical? _____

    _____

Figure 1.8: Resolved! Worksheet

From *Once Upon A Time: Fairy Tales in the Library and Language Arts Classroom for Grades 3-6*, by Jane Heitman. Columbus, OH: Linworth Publishing, Inc. Further reproduction prohibited. Copyright ©2007.

What If?

Supports AASL standards   2, 3, 5, 9
Supports NCTE standards   1, 3, 11, 12

This lesson leads students to think beyond the fairy tale itself, using inference and predicting skills to determine what would happen in circumstances not mentioned in the story. They will also demonstrate story comprehension. Choose a fairy tale. Read it aloud to students or have a student read it aloud to the class. Then ask a "What if" question about plot and characters. The answer to the question should significantly change the outcome of the story. Here are some examples: What if....?

- Cinderella left the ball before midnight and did not leave anything behind?
- Rapunzel's father did not agree with the witch's deal to trade her salad greens for his child?
- The fairy gave Sleeping Beauty the gift of athletic ability rather than the terrible gift of being pricked by a spindle?
- Beauty refused to marry Beast?
- Snow White did not eat the poisoned apple?
- Rumpelstiltskin's name was not discovered?
- Hansel and Gretel did not come upon the witch's house?
- Jack took his cow to market and did not buy beans?

Have students discuss the situation with a partner or in small groups. Each group will report to the class. If you like, hold a class vote on which scenario would be most likely, based on what you know from the rest of the story.

➤ Extended Activity

After students have discussed the question you asked, have them write their own questions for class or small group discussion.

Making Connections

Supports AASL standards   1, 2, 3, 4, 5, 6, 9
Supports NCTE standards   1, 2, 3, 6, 11

This lesson helps students make connections between fairy tales and modern literature and media by considering story elements. They will recognize patterns between the old fairy tales and current culture. They will apply critical thinking to aid their comprehension.

Before doing this lesson, students should have read several fairy tales, as well as other commonly known books. Ask students to name fairy tales. Write the titles on one side of a white board, projected overhead transparency, or projected word processing document. Then ask students to name popular or well-known books, movies, and TV shows appropriate for their age. Write these titles on the other side of the board, transparency, or document.

Next, have students work with partners or in small groups. Each group should choose one of the popular titles and then see which of the fairy tales it is like, if any. Distribute the Making Connections worksheet, Figure 1.9, to guide each group. When the groups have finished, they will report to the class. Ask the class if they agree or disagree with the group's report and why.

▸ Extended Activity

Help students create a readers advisory document, either in print or on a computer file, using the results from Making Connections. Title the document "If You Liked This....Try This," "Fairy Tale Readers Advisory," "Making Connections," or something similar. The contents should be a list linking popular titles to fairy tales. For example, "If you liked the *Harry Potter* books, try (whatever fairy tale they found to be similar)." The list could also link the other way, listing the fairy tale first. For example, "If you liked 'Rumpelstiltskin,' try (whatever popular titles they found to be similar)." Make the document available to students throughout the school, either by printing a copy for the library or by posting it on the school Web site.

Making Connections

Name _____ Date _____

Title of popular book, movie, or TV show we chose
_____

We think the above is like this fairy tale: _____

They are alike because of (check all that apply)

_____ the characters (who are in the story)

_____ the setting (time and place)

_____ the plot (what happens in the story)

_____ the theme (main idea or message)

For the items you checked above, explain how they are alike.

_____
_____
_____
_____
_____
_____
_____
_____
_____
_____
_____
_____
_____
_____

Figure 1.9: Making Connections

From *Once Upon A Time: Fairy Tales in the Library and Language Arts Classroom for Grades 3-6*, by Jane Heitman. Columbus, OH: Linworth Publishing, Inc. Further reproduction prohibited. Copyright ©2007.

Character

Type Them

Supports AASL standards 1, 2, 3, 5, 6, 9
Supports NCTE standards 1, 2, 3, 6, 11

This lesson helps students differentiate between stereotyped and fully developed, well-drawn characters. Students will apply comprehension, context, and pattern recognition skills. Define a "stereotyped character" as a "character representing a sort of person, without individual characteristics." Lead a discussion reviewing fairy tale characters vs. fully developed characters. Most fairy tale characters are stereotypes, not individuals. Most fairy tale characters, even main characters, do not have real names. They are labeled by their role or occupation, such as "Beauty," "Beast," "Prince," "Witch," and "Stepmother." They are one-dimensional, showing only one side of their personalities. Even Hansel and Gretel, named characters, are only one-sided characters representing lost children.

Most good literature contains fully developed characters, especially main characters, who think and act like real people with good and bad qualities. The characters' motivations are made clear by giving characters detailed backgrounds, families, and friendships. Characters' dialogue and thoughts display their individuality. Even good literature stereotypes some minor characters, as the author does not need to develop the characters on the fringe of the story. Ask students what well-developed characters they know from books, movies, or TV. Discuss similarities and differences between these characters and stereotyped characters.

Have students work individually or with a partner to read three different fairy tales. Distribute three copies of Figure 1.10, Type Them, to help students type the characters they have read about. When everyone has completed the assignment, have one student tell one type. Then ask everyone in the class who found that type to stand. They should cross that type off their lists. Have the next student tell another type. All students who found that type should stand. They cross that type off their lists. Continue until there are no more new types. Discuss the results with students by asking what surprised them and what they had expected.

▶ Extended Activity

Have students read a fairy tale and a modernized version of the same tale, such as "Cinderella" and *Ella Enchanted*. They will report to the class on differences in character development between the two versions.

Type Them

Name _____ Date _____

Fairy Tale Title _____

Characters   Type

Figure 1.10: Type Them

From *Once Upon A Time: Fairy Tales in the Library and Language Arts Classroom for Grades 3-6*, by Jane Heitman. Columbus, OH: Linworth Publishing, Inc. Further reproduction prohibited. Copyright ©2007.

Fairy Tale Coat of Arms

Supports AASL standards   1, 2, 3, 5, 6, 9
Supports NCTE standards   1, 3, 6, 8, 11, 12

This lesson allows students artistic expression in analyzing a fairy tale character or family. Students will use comprehension, context, and critical thinking skills. Explain that families in the Middle Ages, especially royalty, used symbols to depict their family values. These symbols acted as a logo, identifying the family and what it stood for. The symbols are called a coat of arms and are placed on shields, banners, and other items that represent the family. Show examples from resources about heraldry to students. Owl & Mouse Educational Software's "How to Make an Authentic Medieval Coat of Arms" is one source.

Ask students to read a fairy tale of their choice. Then have them pick a character or family and create a coat of arms for them. They may use traditional art supplies or computer graphics. Distribute Figure 1.11, Fairy Tale Coat of Arms Template, for students to complete. When everyone is finished, students will show their coats of arms and explain the symbols as they relate to their chosen character. This lesson could also be used as an assessment tool.

Troublesome and Trouble Free Traits

Supports AASL standards   1, 2, 3, 5, 9
Supports NCTE standards   1, 3, 6, 11

This lesson helps students consider the connection between character traits and behavior, character motivation, and plot outcome. These skills will be exercised: comprehension, critical thinking, inference, and predicting skills. Tell students that as you read a fairy tale aloud, they should listen to everything about the main character and decide what traits he or she has. Students can write these down as you read. Before reading the story, you may generate a list of character traits, such as greed, kindness, ambition, laziness, selfishness, selflessness, generosity, hospitality, and goodness. Post the list where the class can see it.

When you are finished reading, ask students these questions:

- What character traits did you notice in the main character?
- What is the character's main trait?
- What trait got the character into trouble and how?
- What trait got the character out of trouble and how?

If students hold differing opinions, help them look for evidence in the story to support their claims.

Next, have students work alone or with a partner. They will read a fairy tale and analyze the main character's traits. Distribute Figure 1.12, Trouble and Traits, to guide them. They will report to the class when they are done.

Fairy Tale Coat of Arms Template

Name _____ Date _____

Fairy Tale Character or Family _____

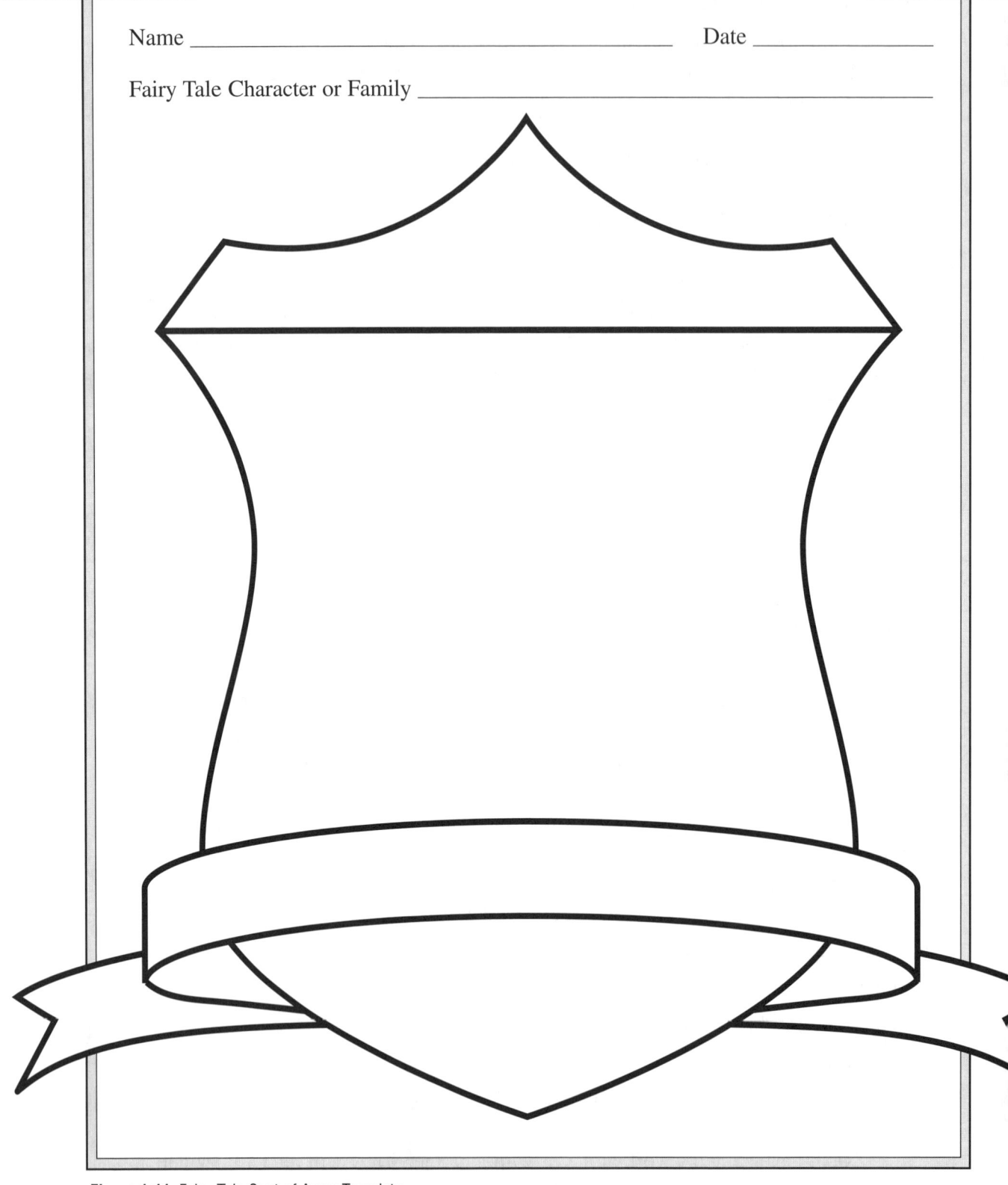

Figure 1.11: Fairy Tale Coat of Arms Template

From *Once Upon A Time: Fairy Tales in the Library and Language Arts Classroom for Grades 3-6*, by Jane Heitman. Columbus, OH: Linworth Publishing, Inc. Further reproduction prohibited. Copyright ©2007.

Trouble and Traits

Name _____ Date _____

Fairy Tale Title _____

Main Character _____

What is the character's main trait?

_____
_____
_____

What trait got the character into trouble and how?

_____
_____
_____

What trait got the character out of trouble and how?

_____
_____
_____

Figure 1.12: Trouble and Traits

From *Once Upon A Time: Fairy Tales in the Library and Language Arts Classroom for Grades 3-6*, by Jane Heitman. Columbus, OH: Linworth Publishing, Inc. Further reproduction prohibited. Copyright ©2007.

How Does the Character Feel?

Supports AASL standards   1, 2, 3, 5, 6, 9
Supports NCTE standards   1, 3, 6, 11

This lesson helps students' inference, comprehension, and predicting skills in considering the main character's emotions. Explain that in good stories, the main character wants something, runs into obstacles in attempting to get it, and matures in the process. The main character's actions and reactions show this growth. Charting a character's emotional response to an event can help students see character growth and identify emotions. You may want to generate a list of emotions for students to use. Ask students to listen for character growth through changing emotions as you read a fairy tale aloud.

Next, go through the story scene by scene and decide together what emotion the main character is feeling. Base your decision on evidence in the text, if possible. If no evidence exists, ask students how they would feel if they were the main character in that situation. Write responses on a white board or other medium for all to see.

Then distribute Figure 1.13, How Does the Character Feel? worksheet. Ask students to read a fairy tale on their own or with a partner and complete the worksheet. They will report to the class when they have finished. Discuss similarities and differences among stories.

Adapt the assignment for special learners or English language learners by having them draw a facial expression to represent an emotion, such as a smiley face for happy.

Setting

Time and Again

Supports AASL standards   1, 2, 3, 5, 6, 9
Supports NCTE standards   1, 3, 6, 11

This lesson focuses students on the importance of the time in which a story takes place. Students will use comprehension, context, inference, and predicting skills. Many fairy tales take place "once upon a time," which is understood to be a vague, long time ago. Tell students that one aspect of setting is time, or when the story takes place. Read a fairy tale aloud, asking students to listen for hints about the tale's time period. When you are finished reading, have students tell you what they think the time period is. They should give information from the tale as evidence. Now ask them how the story would change if it took place in a different time period, such as now or fifty years from now. (If students are studying an historical era in social studies, choose that one.)

Next, have students work in pairs or groups. Distribute Figure 1.14, Time and Again Worksheet. They will choose and read a fairy tale, identifying its time period and giving textual evidence. Then they should choose a different time period and consider how that will alter the story. The groups will report their results to the entire class.

How Does the Character Feel?

Name _____ Date _____

Title of Fairy Tale _____

Main Character _____

Complete the table below by describing actions in the story, the main character's emotion accompanying the action, and why you think the main character felt that way. You may not need all the rows below or you may need more, depending on the story you choose. Use your own words or use the Emotions list at the bottom of the page if you need suggestions.

Action	Emotion	Why I Think So

Emotions
happy	nervous	disturbed	hateful
sad	confident	peaceful	angry
afraid	confused	loving	proud

Figure 1.13: How Does the Character Feel?

From *Once Upon A Time: Fairy Tales in the Library and Language Arts Classroom for Grades 3-6*, by Jane Heitman. Columbus, OH: Linworth Publishing, Inc. Further reproduction prohibited. Copyright ©2007.

Time and Again Worksheet

Name _____ Date _____

Fairy Tale Title _____

Author (if given) _____

Setting (time) _____

Evidence from fairy tale_____

_____

_____

_____

Circle one of the time period settings below that is different from the one you listed above.

200 years in the future   1776   1492   1865

If the fairy tale you read were moved to the setting you circled, how would the story change? Write your answers here. Use more paper if needed.

_____

_____

_____

_____

_____

_____

_____

_____

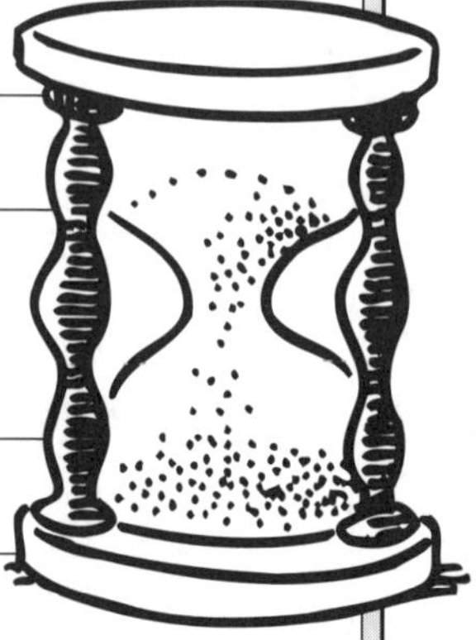

Figure 1.14: Time and Again Worksheet

From *Once Upon A Time: Fairy Tales in the Library and Language Arts Classroom for Grades 3-6*, by Jane Heitman. Columbus, OH: Linworth Publishing, Inc. Further reproduction prohibited. Copyright ©2007.

Replaced Fairy Tales

Supports AASL standards 1, 2, 3, 5, 6, 9
Supports NCTE standards 1, 3, 6, 11

In this lesson, students will learn the impact of where a story takes place. They will use critical thinking, inference, and predicting skills. Explain to students that part of setting is place, where the story happens. Then read a fairy tale aloud. After the story, ask students why the place was important. How did it contribute to the story? Next, ask them to think about what the same story would be like if the action occurred somewhere else. For example, if you read "Hansel and Gretel," ask, "What if the tale took place in a city instead of a forest?"

Then have students, working in pairs or small groups, read a fairy tale. Distribute Figure 1.15, Replaced Fairy Tales, to each group. They should identify the setting and its importance to the tale. Next, they will choose a different setting from among those listed and discuss how that setting would change the story. The groups will report to the class when they are finished.

▶ Extended Activity

Have students create story scenes using computer graphics or traditional art supplies They may even make dioramas. These scenes should show the contrast between the original story and the replacement time period.

Theme

The Big Picture

Supports AASL standards 1, 2, 3, 5, 6, 9
Supports NCTE standards 1, 3, 6, 11

This lesson teaches the literary concept of theme, a difficult concept for elementary students who may not be abstract thinkers yet. Students will use comprehension, critical thinking, and inference skills. The word "theme," in general, is used to mean "motif" or "main idea." In literature, "theme" is not quite as trite as a moral (as in Aesop's fables) or as general as a subject (friendship, for example). It is usually the author's unstated message about life. The theme shows the author's big-picture view of the world. A sample theme might be "the transforming power of friendship."

While fairy tales are known more for their strong plots than for their themes, they do have identifiable themes, usually related to human behavior. For example, a theme of "Cinderella" could be "virtue will be rewarded." (Section I mentions themes more in the general than in the literary sense for the eight selected tales.)

Help students understand theme by listening to the library media specialist or language arts teacher read several fairy tales aloud. After each one, ask, "What's the big picture?" More than one answer can be correct for each story.

Then ask students, working in pairs or groups, to read a fairy tale and identify a theme based on evidence from the story. Distribute Figure 1.16, The Big Picture Worksheet, to guide the groups. Allow special learners or English language learners to develop an artistic representation of the theme. Groups will report to the entire class when everyone is finished. Discuss any differences of opinion.

It's a Classic

Supports AASL standards   1, 2, 3, 5, 6, 8, 9
Supports NCTE standards   1, 3, 6, 7, 8, 9, 11

This lesson investigates what makes a classic a classic. Students will use comprehension, critical thinking, and research skills. Though not strictly related to theme, classic qualities include all story elements, including (and perhaps most important) theme, the universal idea. Ask students to define "classic." They may give answers such as "stands the test of time," or "traditional." These are correct, as is "a standard of excellence." Explain that fairy tales are considered classics because they have lasted for hundreds or thousands of years, depending on the tale. Ask students why that would be. Write their responses on a white board or projected overhead transparency.

Read a fairy tale (preferably an original version or one close to the original) aloud to them. Then ask, "What qualities of this story have made it last?" Add these responses to those already posted on the white board or projected overhead transparency.

Next, working in groups, have students predict what popular contemporary literature will become classics and why, based on the qualities they have identified on the white board or projected overhead transparency. Groups will report to the class. Encourage discussion regarding agreement or disagreement.

➤ *Extended Activity*

Help groups research the history of a fairy tale, using information and resources mentioned in this book, in the library, and on the Internet. Ask groups to find out where and when the fairy tale originated and where it has spread. Have them think about why the tale would come from a particular place and time. Reports can range from simple oral reports, with each group member speaking, or they can be elaborate multimedia productions including maps, other graphics, and sound.

Replaced Fairy Tales

Name _____ Date _____

Fairy Tale Title _____

Author (if given) _____

Setting (place) _____

Effect on story _____

_____

_____

_____

Circle one of the settings below that is different from the one you listed above.

desert

mountains

jungle

seashore

plains

inner city

farm

Arctic or Antarctic

If the fairy tale you read were moved to the setting you circled, how would the story change? Write your answers here. Use more paper if needed.

_____

_____

_____

Figure 1.15: Replaced Fairy Tales

From *Once Upon A Time: Fairy Tales in the Library and Language Arts Classroom for Grades 3-6*, by Jane Heitman. Columbus, OH: Linworth Publishing, Inc. Further reproduction prohibited. Copyright ©2007.

The Big Picture Worksheet

Name _____ Date _____

Title of Fairy Tale _____

Author (if given) _____

What's the big picture (theme)? Write your answer in the picture frame below.

[ ]

What evidence from the story shows this? _____
_____
_____
_____

Figure 1.16: The Big Picture Worksheet

From *Once Upon A Time: Fairy Tales in the Library and Language Arts Classroom for Grades 3-6*, by Jane Heitman. Columbus, OH: Linworth Publishing, Inc. Further reproduction prohibited. Copyright ©2007.

Assessment Suggestions

Some of the previous lessons contain assessment suggestions. Assessments may be formal and informal and include the following:

Fairy Tale Bingo

Supports AASL standards   1, 2, 3, 5, 6, 9
Supports NCTE standards   1, 3, 11

This activity is a good assessment to review students' knowledge of one fairy tale or several. Use the Fairy Tale Bingo template, Figure 1.17. In each box, write a character name or significant place or thing from a fairy tale. You may also use pictures to represent characters, places, and things. Write an accompanying list of 12 to 15 clues for the bingo caller to read. Reproduce and distribute the cards, one per student, and a dozen beans or some other small objects to act as markers. The caller reads a clue. Students decide what or who is being referenced and mark their cards. The first student to mark all the boxes in a row should call "Bingo!" Then check the card to see if the student was correct. If possible, offer a small prize.

See sample clues and a sample card for "Cinderella" below.
Sample card for Cinderella Bingo:

Cinderella	Stepsisters	Stepmother
Prince	Glass slipper	Fairy Godmother
Midnight	*Free*	Father
Ball	Coach	Ashes or Cinders
Horses	Rat	Servant

Figure 1.18: Cinderella Bingo Sample

From *Once Upon A Time: Fairy Tales in the Library and Language Arts Classroom for Grades 3-6*, by Jane Heitman. Columbus, OH: Linworth Publishing, Inc. Further reproduction prohibited. Copyright ©2007.

Fairy Tale Bingo

	Free	

Figure 1.17: Fairy Tale Bingo

From *Once Upon A Time: Fairy Tales in the Library and Language Arts Classroom for Grades 3-6*, by Jane Heitman. Columbus, OH: Linworth Publishing, Inc. Further reproduction prohibited. Copyright ©2007.

Sample Clues for Cinderella Bingo:

1. A good girl mistreated by her family	6. Made Cinderella dress them	10. Showed favoritism to the girls of the house
2. Danced with Cinderella	14. What Cinderella left behind at the party	8. Helped Cinderella get to the party
3. Cinderella's magic wore off at this time	*Free*	4. Often-absent parent
7. Everyone was invited to this party	11. Pumpkin	5. Cinderella got her name because she sat here
13. Mice	12. Coachman	9. Cinderella was treated like this, not as part of the family

✴ Alternate Activity

Instead of the librarian or teacher creating the clues and cards, have students make sets of cards and write their own clues for games to be played by the entire class.

Self Assessment

A student tracks progress on a chart or in a log, journal, folder, or portfolio kept in the classroom or library. Charts and logs track assignments completed. Journals also track the student's perceptions about what he or she has learned. A folder holds all of a student's work for a unit or time period, while a portfolio has more presentation quality. A portfolio contains a student's work, as well as explanatory notes and narrative by the student about his or her work.

Peer Assessment

Peer assessment is best used as a component of presentations. Distribute multiple copies of Figure 1.19, Peer Assessment Template, before group presentations, and ask students who are not presenting to assess their peers' presentations. In addition to students rating their peers, this method keeps all students actively engaged.

Library Media Specialist and Teacher Assessment

Observation and spot-checking students' work are informal assessment methods. Many education professionals use rubrics or contracts to assess their students. These allow students some choice in determining the score for which they want to work. Grades are not a surprise to students, because they know the educator's expectations in advance. A sample rubric follows.

Peer Assessment Template

My name _____ Date _____

Assignment title _____

Student being assessed _____

I am looking and listening for _____

_____

Circle Yes or No for each of the following:

This student followed instructions.	Yes	No
This student showed understanding of the assignment.	Yes	No
This student used appropriate language for the purpose.	Yes	No
This student used appropriate language for the audience.	Yes	No
This student presented with fluency.	Yes	No

I think this student's work was (circle one):

Unsatisfactory   Satisfactory   Excellent

because_____

_____

_____

_____

Other comments:_____

_____

_____

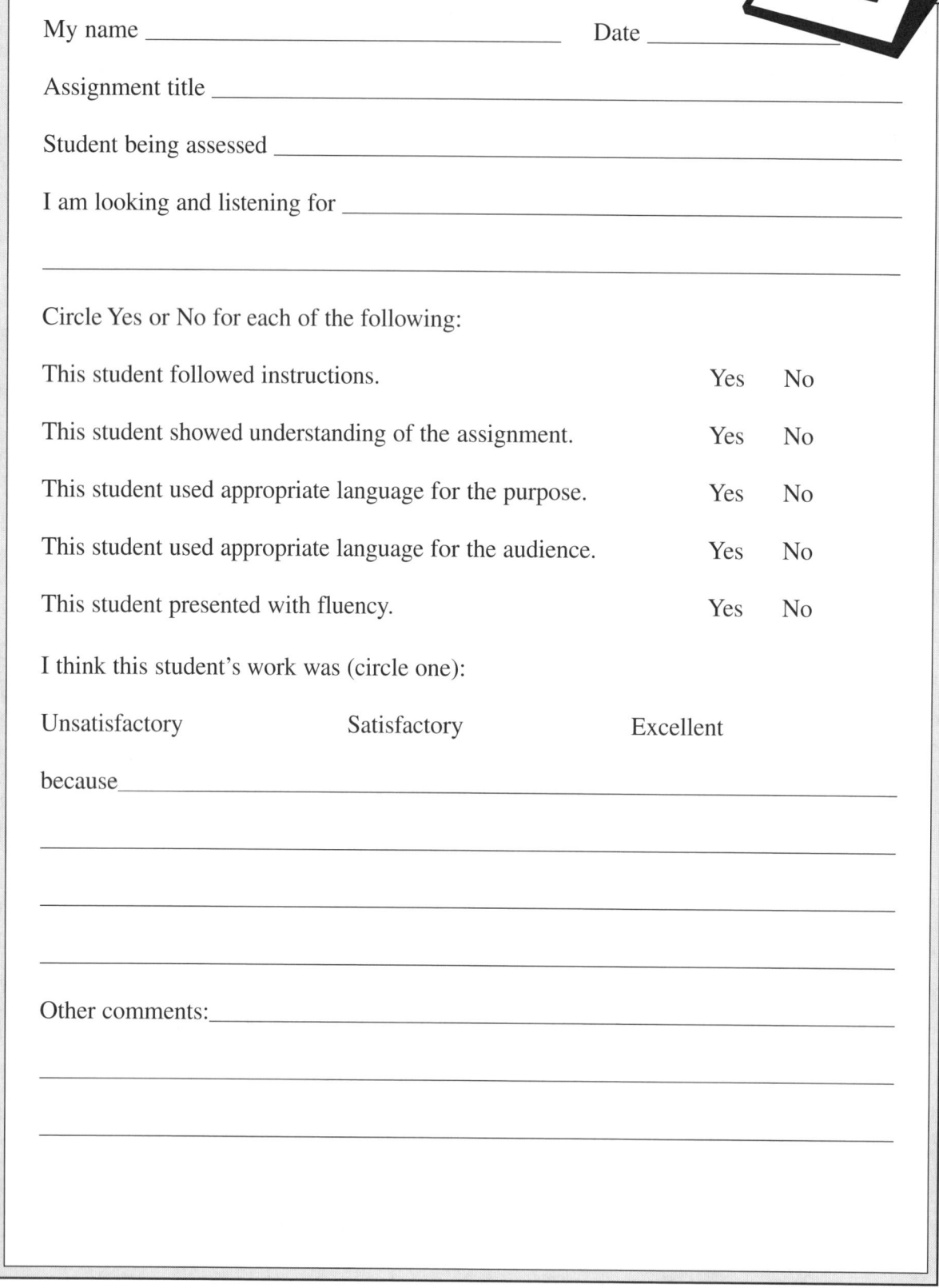

Figure 1.19: Peer Assessment Template

From *Once Upon A Time: Fairy Tales in the Library and Language Arts Classroom for Grades 3-6*, by Jane Heitman. Columbus, OH: Linworth Publishing, Inc. Further reproduction prohibited. Copyright ©2007.

Sample Rubric: Reading Inference

Objectives	Unsatisfactory	Satisfactory	Excellent	Points Earned
Students will use contextual clues to infer what will happen next in the story.	**1 point** Student read the story, but does not find contextual clues and is unable to infer what will happen next.	**5 points** Student read the story, found 1 contextual clue and made an inference.	**10 points** Student read the story, found more than 1 contextual clue, and made a logical inference.	
Student will be able to fluently articulate inference and clues.	**1 point** Student is unable to articulate inference or clues fluently.	**5 points** Student articulates inference or clues with some fluency.	**10 points** Student articulates inference and clues without hesitation.	
			Score	

Figure 1.20 Sample Rubric: Reading, Inference

Assessment Resources:

Fiderer, Adele. *40 Rubrics & Checklists to Assess Reading and Writing: Time-Saving Reproducible Forms and Great Strategies for Meaningful Assessment*. New York: Scholastic, 1999.

Groeber, Joan F. *Designing Rubrics for Reading and Language Arts*. Arlington Heights, IL: SkyLight, 2003.

Nichols, Beverly, et al. *Managing Curriculum and Assessment: A Practitioner's Guide*. Worthington, OH: Linworth, 2006.

Schrock, Kathleen. "Teacher Helpers: Assessment & Rubric Information." *Kathy Schrock's Guide for Educators*. Discovery Education. 02 June 2007 <http://school.discovery.com/schrockguide/assess.html>.

Sullivan, Mary. *75 Language Arts Assessment Tools*. New York: Scholastic, 2003.

Writing
Compare and Contrast

Tales Alike

Supports AASL standards 1, 2, 3, 5, 6, 9
Supports NCTE standards 1, 3, 5, 6, 11

This lesson will help students see similarities between different versions of the same tale and give them practice in writing comparisons. Doing so requires critical thinking and pattern recognition skills. Have each student read two versions of the same fairy tale. Distribute Figure 2.1, Tales Alike, as a planning guide. Explain that comparisons show likenesses or similarities between two things. Then ask students to write an essay about how the tales they read were similar. The library media specialist and language arts teacher can collaborate to decide the requirements of the essay. Requirements will vary depending on the grade and ability level of the students. Younger, less able students can be guided to write a paragraph, while more able students may write five paragraphs. The language arts teacher can provide supplemental material from the language arts text. The finished essays should be read aloud to the class or in small groups.

A good essay has
- An introductory sentence or paragraph that tells what the essay is about.
- One or more paragraphs developing the main idea.
- Each paragraph develops one main point.
- A concluding sentence or paragraph that sums up the main idea.

Resources About Writing Essays

Tompkins, Gail E. *Teaching Writing: Balancing Process and Product.* 4th ed. Upper Saddle River, NJ: Prentice, 2003.
Young, Sue. *Scholastic Guides: Writing with Style.* New York: Scholastic, 1999.

* Alternate Activity

For younger students or students with fewer writing or English language skills, try these ideas:
- Have students complete Figure 2.1, Tales Alike, as their writing assignment
- Have students complete Figure 2.1, Tales Alike, and then work with partners or aides to write their essays
- Have students work with a partner, an aide, or in small groups
- Do the assignment together as a class

Tales Alike

Name _____ Date _____

Use this as a planning guide for your essay.

Title of fairy tale _____

Author (if given) _____

Title of fairy tale _____

Author (if given) _____

In the areas below, write things that are alike in the tales.

Characters	Time & Place of Tale	Story Action

Other alike things I noticed _____

_____

_____

_____

Figure 2.1: Tales Alike

From *Once Upon A Time: Fairy Tales in the Library and Language Arts Classroom for Grades 3-6*, by Jane Heitman. Columbus, OH: Linworth Publishing, Inc. Further reproduction prohibited. Copyright ©2007.

Hooray for Differences

Supports AASL standards 1, 2, 3, 5, 6, 9
Supports NCTE standards 1, 3, 5, 6, 11

This lesson will help students see differences between different versions of the same tale and give them practice in writing contrasts. Students will apply critical thinking and pattern recognition skills. Have each student read two versions of the same fairy tale. Distribute Figure 2.2, Hooray for Differences, as a planning guide. Explain that contrasts show differences between two things. Then ask students to write an essay about how the tales they read were different. The finished essays will be published in a class newsletter.

✱ Alternate Activity

For younger students or students with fewer writing or English language skills, try these ideas:

- Have students complete Figure 2.2, Hooray for Differences, as their writing assignment
- Have students complete Figure 2.2, Hooray for Differences, and then work with partners or aides to write their essays
- Have students work with a partner, an aide, or in small groups
- Do the assignment together as a class
- Have students draw pictures to show alike and different

Writing Story Elements

Plot

What Could Happen Next?

Supports AASL standards 1, 2, 3, 5, 6, 9
Supports NCTE standards 1, 3, 5, 6, 7, 11, 12

This sequencing lesson requires creative critical thinking and predicting skills, as students consider possibilities for plot twists. Most stories are comprised of scenes in which the action happens. In each scene of rising action, the author must keep the main character from reaching his or her goal. Each scene becomes more and more dramatic.

To accomplish this, writers often brainstorm potential possible obstacles and choose the one that makes the most sense at that point in the story, but also adds a bit of surprise. Choose a fairy tale to read aloud to the class. Decide in advance where crucial action takes place, and stop reading aloud at that point. Then ask the class, "What could happen next?" Write responses on the board or projected overhead transparency. Continue reading and compare the fairy tale plot to the students' suggestions. Read again until just before the next crucial action and repeat asking, recording, reading, and comparing. Leave all recordings on the board, to be used later. Continue until the tale is finished. Discuss whether the tale contained any surprises, whether it is believable, and whether the outcome was satisfying. Even fairy tale worlds must be constructed believably.

Next ask students to rewrite the tale, beginning with the tale's beginning, but changing the story by using one or more of the ideas from their predictions. Students may work individually or in groups. When everyone is finished, students will read their tales aloud in small groups. Distribute and have students complete Figure 2.3, What Could Happen Next? Evaluation to assess each other's stories. Conclude by conducting a general class discussion about what the students learned.

Tag Team Tales

Supports AASL standards   2, 3, 5, 6, 9
Supports NCTE standards   1, 3, 4, 5, 6, 11, 12

Students will express creative critical thinking abilities while focusing on sequencing in this lesson. Before beginning this lesson, students should be familiar with a variety of fairy tales. You may review some of the common traits of fairy tales, such as royal characters and magic. Place students in small groups. Give each group one sheet of ruled paper per person. Tell students that when you say "Once upon a time," everyone should write that phrase on the top of their paper and complete the sentence. Then they should pass their papers to the right. Students will read what is written on the paper and write the next sentence or two. Then they should pass their papers to the right, and continue writing and passing. After a specified time has passed, say, "And they lived happily ever after" to conclude. Students should write that sentence at the end of their tales.

Have students read their tales among their groups. Ask them to listen for logical sequencing. Ask whether the tales progressed as the originator expected. Then have each group choose one story to read to the entire class.

✽ Alternate Activity

Rather than passing their papers, designate one student as the scribe. The scribe will write down each person's oral addition to the story.

Hooray for Differences

Name _____ Date _____

Use this as a planning guide for your essay.

Title of fairy tale _____

Author (if given) _____

Title of fairy tale _____

Author (if given) _____

In the areas below, write things that are different in the tales.

Characters	Time & Place of Tale	Story Action

Other differences I noticed _____

_____

_____

_____

Figure 2.2: Hooray for Differences

From *Once Upon A Time: Fairy Tales in the Library and Language Arts Classroom for Grades 3-6*, by Jane Heitman. Columbus, OH: Linworth Publishing, Inc. Further reproduction prohibited. Copyright ©2007.

What Could Happen Next? Evaluation

Name _____ Date _____

Evaluate your groups' tales by completing the chart below.

Tale Writer's Name	Is the Tale Believable and Why?	Is the Outcome Satisfying and Why?	Was There Suprise and If So What?

Figure 2.3: What Could Happen Next? Evaluation

From *Once Upon A Time: Fairy Tales in the Library and Language Arts Classroom for Grades 3-6*, by Jane Heitman. Columbus, OH: Linworth Publishing, Inc. Further reproduction prohibited. Copyright ©2007.

Beyond Once Upon A Time Assessment

Name _____ Date _____

Write your classmates' names in the "Author" column. Listen for traits of a good beginning. Put a check mark in the proper box when you hear the trait.

Author	Main Character	Where Story Happens	When Story Happens	Main Character's Problem

Figure 2.4: Beyond Once Upon A Time Assessment

From *Once Upon A Time: Fairy Tales in the Library and Language Arts Classroom for Grades 3-6*, by Jane Heitman. Columbus, OH: Linworth Publishing, Inc. Further reproduction prohibited. Copyright ©2007.

Beyond Once Upon a Time

Supports AASL standards   1, 2, 3, 5, 6, 9
Supports NCTE standards   1, 3, 4, 5, 6, 11

This lesson gives students practice writing a good story beginning. They will apply comprehension and critical thinking skills. Ask students how most fairy tales begin or have them read the first two paragraphs of several tales. Ask, "What information did you find?" Tell students that good story beginnings (the first paragraph or two) usually introduce the following:

- The main character
- Where the story happens
- When the story happens
- The main character's problem that will move the plot

Ask students to write a good beginning to an original fairy tale. When they are done, they will read their beginnings in groups or to the class. Distribute Figure 2.4, Beyond Once Upon A Time Assessment. The listeners will use it to evaluate which traits of good beginnings are included in each beginning they hear.

▶ Extended Activity

If students' beginnings lack one or more of the traits, encourage them to rewrite their beginnings so that all or most of the traits are included.

New Beginnings

Supports AASL standards   1, 2, 3, 4, 5, 6, 9
Supports NCTE standards   1, 3, 4, 5, 6, 11, 12

This lesson exercises students' creative critical thinking and story structure skills in writing a better beginning than "Once upon a time." Have students look at the first paragraph or two of several fairy tales or read them aloud to the class. Explain to students that in modern writing, authors strive for strong, original beginnings that grab and hold the reader. "Once upon a time" is fine for fairy tales, but modern stories demand something less clichéd. Typical ways to begin stories are

- Description of character
  (such as, "Zelda's blue dress hung on her thin body like a sack, but her smile flashed at her friends.")

- Description of setting
  (such as, "Oswald's thatched-roof hut sat at a crossroads five miles from the Blue Kingdom and five miles from the Red Kingdom.")

- Dialogue
  (such as, "Zelda, quit standing there smiling and go mend the thatch on the roof," Oswald demanded.)

- Main character introducing self
  (such as, "I'm Zelda. I'm skinny and bony from working so hard. Still, it's not a bad life as long as I can smile at my friends.")

- Problem
  (such as, "Just as Oswald and Zelda took their first bite of dinner, their thatched roof fell in, covering their dinner plates, their heads, and their floor with dirt and straw.")

Read a fairy tale beginning and ask students to identify the introductory elements. Then ask them to state a first sentence using each of the methods listed previously.
   Ask each student to choose and read a traditional fairy tale. Distribute Figure 2.5, New Beginnings. They should identify which introductory elements are present. Then they will write an original beginning using one of the methods explained above. They should include as many introductory elements as possible. When they are finished, they will read their beginnings aloud in small groups. Listeners should try to guess which fairy tale provided the basis for the students' original beginnings.

New Beginnings

Name _____ Date _____

Title of fairy tale I read _____

Author (if given) _____

Circle below the items of information contained in the first two paragraphs of the tale.

the main character   *where the story happens*   *when the story happens*

the main character's problem that will move the plot

Write an original beginning to the tale including as many of the items above as you can. Use one of these methods: Description of character, Description of setting, Dialogue, Main character introducing self, Problem.

_____

_____

_____

_____

_____

_____

_____

_____

_____

_____

_____

_____

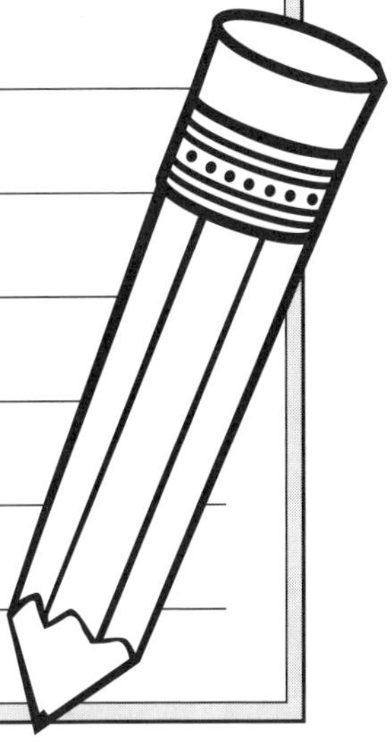

Figure 2.5: New Beginnings

From *Once Upon A Time: Fairy Tales in the Library and Language Arts Classroom for Grades 3-6*, by Jane Heitman. Columbus, OH: Linworth Publishing, Inc. Further reproduction prohibited. Copyright ©2007.

Conflict Makes the Tale

Supports AASL standards   1, 2, 3, 5, 6, 9
Supports NCTE standards   1, 3, 4, 5, 6, 11

Types of Conflict
- Character against character
- Character against nature
- Character against self
- Character against society

This lesson develops students' comprehension and predicting skills. Though a problem is introduced in a tale's beginning, it is the heart of the tale's middle. The plot, the tale's action, depends on the main character running into obstacle after obstacle. Problems and obstacles are called "conflict" in the story. For more details about conflict, see Confounded Conflict in the Reading section of this book.

After you have discussed conflict with students, read aloud a fairy tale. Ask them to identify the conflict and find examples throughout the tale. Next, ask students how the story would change if the conflict were a different type. For example, if the tale you read was character against character, how would the story differ with character against nature conflict instead? The ending may still be "happily ever after," but the rest of the story may be completely different.

Distribute Figure 2.6, Conflict Makes the Tale. Students will read a fairy tale of their choice and identify the conflict. Then they will write the story with a different type of conflict. When they are finished, students will make their stories into illustrated books, using traditional art supplies or computer graphics.

Obstacle Course

Supports AASL standards   1, 2, 3, 4, 5, 6, 9
Supports NCTE standards   1, 3, 5, 6, 11, 12

Conflict involves the obstacles the main characters face to reach their goals. This lesson teaches skills in comprehension, identifying the main action, and story structure. Read aloud a fairy tale to students. Ask what the main character wants. Then write on the board or projected overhead transparency the obstacles that keep the character from that goal.

Distribute Figure 2.7, Obstacle Course, to students as a planning guide. Have them make up a character, character's goal, and three obstacles. Students will write their own fairy tales based on that information. Publish the fairy tales in a class newsletter in hard copy, on disks for each student, or in a computer file.

Conflict Makes the Tale

Name _____ Date _____

Title of fairy tale I read _____

Author (if given) _____

Circle the correct conflict type.

Character against character   *Character against nature*

Character against self   *Character against society*

Example from the tale _____

Choose a different conflict type and rewrite the tale on your own paper.

Conflict type I chose _____

_____

Figure 2.6: Conflict Makes the Tale

From *Once Upon A Time: Fairy Tales in the Library and Language Arts Classroom for Grades 3-6*, by Jane Heitman. Columbus, OH: Linworth Publishing, Inc. Further reproduction prohibited. Copyright ©2007.

Obstacle Course

Name _____ Date _____

Make up a character with a goal.

Character's name _____

Character's goal _____

Write an obstacle your character meets on each of the obstacles below.

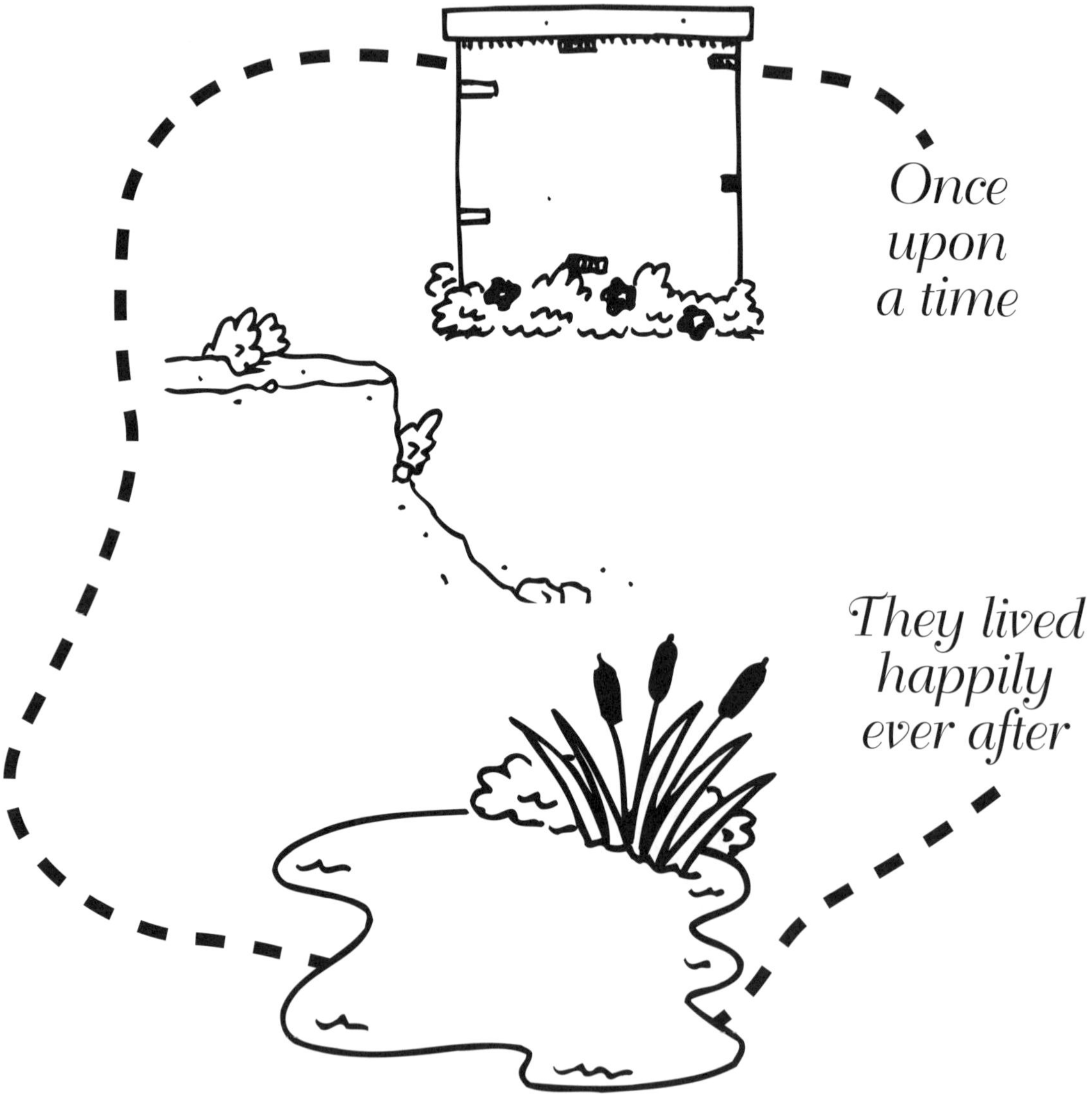

Once upon a time

They lived happily ever after

Use the information above to write an original fairy tale on your own paper. Begin with "Once upon a time" and end with "They lived happily ever after."

Figure 2.7: Obstacle Course

From *Once Upon A Time: Fairy Tales in the Library and Language Arts Classroom for Grades 3-6,* by Jane Heitman. Columbus, OH: Linworth Publishing, Inc. Further reproduction prohibited. Copyright ©2007.

Good Endings

Supports AASL standards 1, 2, 3, 5, 6, 9
Supports NCTE standards 1, 3, 4, 5, 6, 11

In this lesson students will employ good plot resolution techniques by using critical thinking, predicting, and story structure skills. Explain to students that a good story ending (the last paragraph or page) wraps up the plot in a satisfying way, logically and completely. Each of the main characters should be accounted for. The main character's problem is usually resolved in his or her favor, with hints given throughout the plot. If the main character's problem is not resolved in his or her favor, the reason must be clear and believable, also hinted at throughout the plot.

Ask students what the usual fairy tale ending is, and they will respond, "Happily ever after." Other issues are resolved, too. For example, Cinderella and the prince live happily ever after, but what happens to the stepmother and stepsisters depends on which version is read. Most versions do tell what happens to them, happy or not.

Read aloud a fairy tale to the class, stopping before the end. Ask the following questions, inviting their evidence from the text for their predictions:

- How do you think the main character's problem will be solved?
- How do you think the main character grows emotionally from the beginning of the story to the end?
- What do you think happens to the other characters?

Then read the ending. How did students' predictions match the author's ending? If predictions did not match the ending, point out that the students were not necessarily wrong. The ending was simply the one the author chose. Ask students why they think the author chose that ending. Do they prefer one of their own ideas or the author's and why? Did students find the ending satisfying? Is the main character's problem solved in a logical way? Ask if all the characters' actions have been resolved. Could the ending be improved and still be logical?

Now read another fairy tale aloud and stop before the ending. Distribute Figure 2.8, Good Endings. Have each student write an ending, using Figure 2.8 as a guide. When they are done, they will read their endings aloud in small groups. You may distribute Figure 2.9, Good Endings Assessment, for students to use as assessment tools in their groups. Less able students or English language learners may illustrate their endings rather than writing them. They may also speak and record their endings. A partner, aide, or teacher can help them write it from their recording.

When the groups have completed their tasks, read the ending to the fairy tale. See how many students were close to the original ending. Ask volunteers to read their endings to the class.

Good Endings

Name _____ Date _____

A good ending:

- *is satisfying*
- *is logical*
- *solves the main character's problem*
- *shows emotional growth of main character*
- *tells what happens to other characters*

Write your ending here: _____

_____

_____

_____

_____

_____

_____

_____

_____

_____

_____

_____

Figure 2.8: Good Endings

From *Once Upon A Time: Fairy Tales in the Library and Language Arts Classroom for Grades 3-6*, by Jane Heitman. Columbus, OH: Linworth Publishing, Inc. Further reproduction prohibited. Copyright ©2007.

Good Endings Assessment

Name of assesssor _____   Date _____

Name of author_____

Put a check mark beside each of the good ending traits that you hear and explain why you did or did not check a trait.

This ending

_____is satisfying. Why or why not?_____

_____

_____is logical. Why or why not?_____

_____

_____solves the main character's problem. Why or why not?_____

_____

_____shows emotional growth of main character. Why or why not?_____

_____

_____tells what happens to other characters. Why or why not?_____

_____

Other comments_____

_____

_____

_____

_____

Figure 2.9: Good Endings Assessment

From *Once Upon A Time: Fairy Tales in the Library and Language Arts Classroom for Grades 3-6*, by Jane Heitman. Columbus, OH: Linworth Publishing, Inc. Further reproduction prohibited. Copyright ©2007.

You Said It

Supports AASL standards   1, 2, 3, 5, 6, 8, 9
Supports NCTE standards   1, 3, 4, 5, 6, 8, 11, 12

This lesson allows students to use their creative critical thinking skills and write dialogue to move the plot. Students will also identify the main action of the story. Introduce or reinforce "dialogue" by defining it as "what people say to each other." Dialogue is a fast, interesting way to move the plot forward. It also tells us about the characters. The way they speak reveals their motivations, education, and status, which all have an impact on the plot. You may use graphic novels as an example.

Choose and read aloud a scene from a fairy tale. Then, as a class, make a graphic, or cartoon, version of the scene on the board or on a projected overhead transparency. Use stick figures for characters if need be. Ask students what the character would say and write it in a speech bubble pointing to the character. Continue through the scene.

Have students create graphic versions of a fairy tale scene or entire tale of their choice, working individually or in groups. They will present their work to the class when they are finished. They may present their dialogues as a play, or they may create and project a graphic novel using computer graphics software. The audience should listen for how the dialogue moves the plot forward and whether the speech represents the character accurately.

Fairy Tale Tribune

Supports AASL standards   1, 2, 3, 5, 6, 8, 9
Supports NCTE standards   1, 3, 5, 6, 7, 11

Students will practice journalistic writing in this lesson. They will apply comprehension, critical thinking, and story structure skills. Before class, gather enough newspapers for each student. Distribute them to students and give them time to read a news story or two. Ask how this writing is different from the writing in fairy tales or other stories. Journalistic writing for straight news stories contains only the necessary facts. The most important information appears in the first paragraph and includes the answers to these questions: who?, what?, when?, where?, why?, and how?

Tell the class they will write and publish an issue of the *Fairy Tale Tribune* newspaper. Create a newspaper template using word processing or desktop publishing software. Working with partners, students should choose a fairy tale and write a news story based on the tale. Check their finished story for errors or assign an "editor" to this task. Allow students to revise as needed and key the story into the template.

Newspapers use graphics and photographs, so allow some students to choose or design appropriate illustrations and write captions for them.

When all the groups have finished, print copies of the *Fairy Tale Tribune* for the class. Post the newspaper to your school Web site, if you like.

▶ Extended Activity

Have a representative from your local newspaper talk to the class about journalism or take a field trip to the newspaper office or share the *Fairy Tale Tribune* with younger students.

You're Invited

Supports AASL standards 1, 2, 3, 5, 6, 9
Supports NCTE standards 3, 4, 5, 6, 11

In this lesson, students will apply comprehension and inference skills. After students have become familiar with several fairy tales, distribute Figure 2.10, You're Invited Template. Have students choose a fairy tale and write an invitation to an event from one character to another on the template. The event may actually be part of the story, such as the prince inviting Cinderella's family to the ball, or imaginary but text-based, such as the dwarfs inviting Snow White to live with them. When students have completed their templates, students will present them in small groups and display them in the classroom.

Write Original Fairy Tale

Supports AASL standards 1, 2, 3, 5, 6, 9
Supports NCTE standards 3, 4, 5, 6, 11, 12

This lesson allows students to use their creativity and employ a fairy tale format. They will use comprehension, pattern recognition, and story structure skills. After students have read several fairy tales, discuss fairy tale format with them. What traits do fairy tales have in common? Write a list on the board or projected overhead transparency. When your list is complete, have students write an original fairy tale, using the traits they have identified as a format guide. When they are finished they will share their stories in small groups. Group members will listen for the required traits.

You're Invited Template

Name _____ Date _____

Fairy Tale Title _____

Invitation from _____ to _____

for (event) _____

You're Invited!

_____ invites _____
      (Host)   (person being invited)

to _____
                    (event)

on _____
                   (day, date, and time)

at _____
                    (place)

for _____
                   (occasion)

Figure 2.10: You're Invited Template

From *Once Upon A Time: Fairy Tales in the Library and Language Arts Classroom for Grades 3-6*, by Jane Heitman. Columbus, OH: Linworth Publishing, Inc. Further reproduction prohibited. Copyright ©2007.

Fractured Fairy Tale

Supports AASL standards 1, 2, 3, 4, 5, 6, 8, 9
Supports NCTE standards 1, 3, 5, 6, 8, 11, 12

Students will write humorous adaptations of well-known fairy tales in this lesson. They will exercise their comprehension, critical thinking, and story structure skills. After students have read several fairy tales, read a fractured fairy tale to them. Fractured fairy tales are tales that have been twisted in some way to give the story a funny surprise. The alteration may come from changing a character, setting, or plot element. Read to the class an example or two of fractured fairy tales, such as Jon Scieszka's *The True Story of the 3 Little Pigs by A. Wolf* and *The Stinky Cheese Man & Other Fairly Stupid Tales* or Vivian Vande Velde's *Tales from the Brothers Grimm and the Sisters Weird*. When you have read them, ask students what is "fractured" about these tales? This lesson demonstrates the impact theme makes on a story.

Ask students to work individually or with partners to choose a standard fairy tale and write a fractured version of it. They will read their tales to the class, to a younger class who is familiar with the original tales, or to parents and friends. They may also publish their fractured tales in a class newsletter or post on the school Web site, and recommend original versions of the tales.

* Alternate Activity

Use the information and activities at the *Fractured Fairy Tales & Fables with Jon Scieszka* Web site (http://teacher.scholastic.com/writewit/mff/fractured_fairy.htm) where students can publish their fractured tales online.

Script It

Supports AASL standards 1, 2, 3, 5, 6, 9
Supports NCTE standards 1, 3, 4, 5, 6, 11

This lesson emphasizes the importance of dialogue to move a story and teaches students script format. Students will use comprehension, critical thinking, and story structure skills. Before class, locate children's play scripts to distribute to students or project so all can see. Free scripts are available from a variety of online sources, including *Scripts for Schools* and Aaron Shepard's Web site.

After students have read several fairy tales, show them the scripts and ask them what differs between the tales they have read and the script. They should notice that the script is almost entirely dialogue, while the tale is almost entirely narrative. They should also notice that the tale is written in paragraphs that flow from one to another. The script is written in lines with the speaker's name in front of them. Next, have students work with partners or in small groups to choose a fairy tale and rewrite it in script format. If possible, produce it as readers theater, puppet theater, or a regular play. See Section III of this book, Speaking and Listening, for more information.

From Fairy Tale to Fact

Supports AASL standards   1, 2, 3, 4, 5, 6, 8, 9
Supports NCTE standards   1, 2, 3, 4, 5, 6, 7, 8, 11, 12

This lesson helps students use critical thinking, comprehension, and research skills about fiction in relation to fact and gives them practice writing nonfiction. Read a fairy tale aloud to students. Then have students generate a list of nonfiction writing ideas based on the tale. To begin, ask, "What are some things in the story you would like to know more about?" Write the list on the board or a projected overhead transparency. For example, if you read "Hansel and Gretel," nonfiction ideas could include finding information on the following:

- Forests in Germany
- How to make gingerbread houses
- Wilderness survival techniques
- The type of birds in German forests
- Children living in poverty
- How to chop wood
- Brother-sister relationships

Ask students to choose one of the topics from the list or a topic of their own related to the story. Distribute Figure 2.11, From Fairy Tale to Fact Planning Sheet, for students to use as a research and planning guide. Then they should research their topics using library print and online resources, with the help of the library media specialist, as needed. From their research, students will write a report about what they found and present the report to the class.

Poetic Fairy Tales

Supports AASL standards   1, 2, 3, 5, 6, 9
Supports NCTE standards   1, 3, 4, 5, 6, 11

In this lesson, students show comprehension of a fairy tale and use critical thinking to rewrite the tale in a poetic form. After students have read several fairy tales, have students choose one and rewrite the story as a poem, rap, or song. When they are finished, students will recite or perform their work for the class. For more information on classroom poetry writing, see Jane Heitman's *Rhymes and Reasons: Using Poetry to Foster Literacy*. For more about the craft of poetry writing, see books by Ralph Fletcher and Paul Janeczko.

From Fairy Tale to Fact Planning Sheet

Name _____ Date _____

My topic is _____

1. _____
2. _____
3. _____

Notes about what I learned:

_____
_____
_____
_____
_____
_____
_____
_____
_____
_____
_____
_____
_____
_____
_____

Now use complete sentences and paragraphs to write a report based on what you learned.

Figure 2.11: From Fairy Tale to Fact Planning Sheet

From *Once Upon A Time: Fairy Tales in the Library and Language Arts Classroom for Grades 3-6*, by Jane Heitman. Columbus, OH: Linworth Publishing, Inc. Further reproduction prohibited. Copyright ©2007.

Cook It Up!

Supports AASL standards   1, 2, 3, 4, 5, 6, 8, 9
Supports NCTE standards   1, 3, 4, 5, 6, 8, 11, 12

This lesson employs students' creative and critical thinking, inference, and research skills. After students have read several fairy tales, show them sample recipes from books in the library or a Web site, such as *Recipes.com*. Discuss the recipe format and distribute Figure 2.12, Cook It Up! Template. Ask students to choose a fairy tale and write a recipe based on something in the tale. These could be real recipes, such as a gingerbread recipe from "Hansel and Gretel," or silly recipes, such as poisoned apple pie from "Snow White." Special learners or English language learners may use pictures to depict ingredients.

Publish the results in a class booklet or computer file Fairy Tale Cookbook. Conclude the activity by reading aloud from *Fairy Tale Feasts: A Literary Cookbook for Young Readers and Eaters* by Jane Yolen. If school policy allows, make and eat some of the recipes as a celebration of the students' work with fairy tales.

Character

Character Acrostic

Supports AASL standards   1, 2, 3, 5, 6, 8, 9
Supports NCTE standards   1, 3, 4, 5, 6, 11

This lesson poetically displays students' comprehension of fairy tale characters and allows them to employ creative and critical thinking skills. Have each student choose a favorite fairy tale character. Then have students write an acrostic poem using the character's name vertically and adjectives about the character horizontally. Write one together as a class first for practice.

For example:

- Gretel (from "Hansel and Gretel")
- Girl
- Ready
- Enterprising
- Triumphant
- Efficient
- Lost

Students may write their poems on paper or on the computer using a word processing program. They may decorate them with traditional art supplies or graphics software. Have students present them to the class and explain why they chose the words they did. Display the poems in the classroom when they are completed.

Cook It Up! Template

Name _____ Date _____

Recipe

Recipe Title _____

from this fairy tale title_____

Ingredients: _____

_____

_____

How to make it:_____

_____

_____

_____

_____

_____

_____

_____

_____

_____

_____

Serves how many:_____

Figure 2.12: Cook It Up! Template

From *Once Upon A Time: Fairy Tales in the Library and Language Arts Classroom for Grades 3-6*, by Jane Heitman. Columbus, OH: Linworth Publishing, Inc. Further reproduction prohibited. Copyright ©2007.

Wanted–Enchanted or Not

Supports AASL standards   1, 2, 3, 5, 6, 9
Supports NCTE standards   1, 3, 4, 5, 6, 11

This lesson focuses on characters' physical descriptions, and uses students' comprehension and inference skills. If possible, obtain a real Wanted poster or find a facsimile of one on the Internet or other resource. Show it to students and note that the poster lists everything necessary to identify the person by sight. Distribute Figure 2.13, Wanted—Enchanted or Not, and have students create a Wanted poster for a fairy tale villain of their choice after reading at least one fairy tale. They should include a picture they drew, found, or created using a computer program. When everyone is finished, have students present their posters in small groups or to the entire class. Discuss the posters' accuracy based on what the class knows about the character. Refer to the tale to settle any disputes. Display the posters around the room.

▶ Extended Activity

Have students use the information they generated on their Wanted poster as the basis for a paragraph or short essay describing the character.

Character Profile

Supports AASL standards   1, 2, 3, 5, 6, 8, 9
Supports NCTE standards   1, 3, 4, 5, 6, 11

Students learn writing profile basics in this lesson, where they will apply comprehension, inference, and story structure skills. Ask students to read a profile article (an article featuring a person) from an appropriate magazine or read an article aloud to them. Ask what they notice about how profiles are different from other kinds of articles. Most profiles try to show their subject positively and focus on one aspect of the subject's life. Profiles give background on how people got where they are today and why. They include quotes from the person, and often from family, friends, and business associates. Unless profiles are of historical figures, they are usually based on interviews with the subjects.

    Tell students that they are being hired by *Fairy Tale Faces* magazine. They must choose a fairy tale character and write a profile for the magazine. Discuss the kinds of information to include. Distribute Figure 2.14, Character Profile Planning Sheet, as a planning guide. Have students read their completed profiles in small groups or compile them into an actual magazine or e-zine (online magazine).

Wanted—Enchanted or Not

Name _____   Date _____

WANTED—ENCHANTED OR NOT

NAME _____

KNOWN ALIAS _____

SEX _____ **AGE** _____ **RACE** _____

HAIR COLOR _____

EYE COLOR _____

HEIGHT _____

WEIGHT _____

OTHER IDENTIFYING MARKS OR CHARACTERISTICS

_____

_____

WANTED FOR _____

LAST SEEN (place) _____

WEARING _____

REWARD _____

DANGER LEVEL _____

Figure 2.13: Wanted—Enchanted or Not

From *Once Upon A Time: Fairy Tales in the Library and Language Arts Classroom for Grades 3-6*, by Jane Heitman. Columbus, OH: Linworth Publishing, Inc. Further reproduction prohibited. Copyright ©2007.

Character Profile Planning Sheet

Name _____ Date _____

You have been hired by *Fairy Tale Faces* magazine to write a profile about a fairy tale character. Complete the blanks below. Then use your answers to write the profile.

Fairy Tale Character _____

Address _____

Family _____

Most known for _____

Physical characteristics _____
_____

Personality traits _____
_____

Friends _____

Enemies _____

Likes to do these things _____
_____

Quotes from the tale _____
_____
_____

Figure 2.14: Character Profile Planning Sheet

From *Once Upon A Time: Fairy Tales in the Library and Language Arts Classroom for Grades 3-6*, by Jane Heitman. Columbus, OH: Linworth Publishing, Inc. Further reproduction prohibited. Copyright ©2007.

Who Am I?

Supports AASL standards   1, 2, 3, 5, 6, 9
Supports NCTE standards   1, 3, 4, 5, 6, 11

This lesson helps students apply comprehension skills as they strive for accuracy in fairy tale knowledge and writing character descriptions using a guessing game approach. After students have read several fairy tales, have them choose a character and write a description of him or her. The description should NOT name the character, but should describe both physical and personality traits.

When everyone is done, students will read their descriptions in small groups or to the entire class. If the audience guesses the character correctly, the writer has done well.

Fairy Tale Character Resumé

Supports AASL standards   1, 2, 3, 5, 6, 8, 9
Supports NCTE standards   1, 3, 4, 5, 6, 7, 8, 11

When people look for a job, they usually give their employer a resumé that shows their work history and level of responsibility on the job. This lesson helps students apply creative critical thinking and inference about characters and introduces resumé writing skills. Students should have read several fairy tales before beginning this lesson.

Show students sample resumés as found in books and Internet resources, such as *Monster.com*. Discuss the contents and formats of the samples. Distribute Figure 2.15, Fairy Tale Resumé, for students to complete for a fairy tale character of their choice. To be accurate, students must stay true to the fairy tale character, while applying creativity. Students may use computer word processing to finish their resumés.

When everyone is finished, students will share their resumés in small groups. The groups will discuss whether they would hire a character for his job objective and why.

Fairy Tale Resumé

Name _____ Date _____

Complete the blanks to help your fairy tale character get the job he or she wants.

Name of character _____

Address of character _____

_____

Telephone number _____

E-mail address _____

Job goal _____

Experience

_____

_____

_____

_____

_____

Education

_____

_____

_____

_____

_____

Figure 2.15: Fairy Tale Resumé

From *Once Upon A Time: Fairy Tales in the Library and Language Arts Classroom for Grades 3-6*, by Jane Heitman. Columbus, OH: Linworth Publishing, Inc. Further reproduction prohibited. Copyright ©2007.

It's My Business

Supports AASL standards   1, 2, 3, 4, 5, 6, 8, 9
Supports NCTE standards   1, 3, 4, 5, 6, 7, 8, 11

This lesson teaches students the elements and purpose of a business card and helps them analyze fairy tale characters. They will use comprehension, critical thinking, and inference skills. Before this lesson, students should have read several fairy tales. To prepare, collect a variety of business cards from the community. Distribute the cards to students and explain that business people give cards to prospective customers to present themselves and their businesses professionally. Ask students what information they see on the cards. Most business cards have

- The name of the business
- The name of the owner, manager, or representative if different from the business
- Address
- Telephone number
- Fax number
- E-mail address
- Web site address

Many business cards also include graphics, such as a logo, a motto, and short description of types of services.

Distribute to students Figure 2.16, It's My Business Template. Have them choose a fairy tale character and create an appropriate business card for him or her. For example, Cinderella's card could feature a cleaning business. Students should cut them out and exchange them in small groups.

✱ Alternate Activity

Create a business card template in a computer word processing program, or use one that the software provides. Students can make their business cards using the template, saving them in their own files.

It's My Business Template

Name _____ Date _____

Choose a fairy tale character. Think about what business he or she would be in. Then design a business card. Include the character's name, business name, address, telephone number, fax number, e-mail address, and services offered. Draw a logo or graphic if you like.

Figure 2.16: It's My Business Template

From *Once Upon A Time: Fairy Tales in the Library and Language Arts Classroom for Grades 3-6*, by Jane Heitman. Columbus, OH: Linworth Publishing, Inc. Further reproduction prohibited. Copyright ©2007.

Add a Character

Supports AASL standards   1, 2, 3, 5, 6, 9
Supports NCTE standards   1, 3, 5, 6, 11

This lesson exercises students' inference, story structure, and writing skills. Discuss with students what difference it makes what characters are in the story and what characters are not. Read a fairy tale to students. Then ask, "What if we added a character?" Choose a character to add (such as a relative of a character, a shop keeper, a tourist, or a servant). Where would this person fit into the plot? How does the plot change? Discuss the answers and write responses on the board or projected overhead transparency. Ask for sample story sentences including the new character.

    Working in pairs or small groups, students will choose a fairy tale and select a character to add to the tale. They will write the tale with the added character and read their work to the class when they are finished. They should be able to tell how the plot was changed by adding the character they did.

    To conclude this lesson, read one of the following books or another book that contains characters from several stories, or ask students to read one of these on their own.

> Child, Lauren. *Who's Afraid of the Big Bad Book?*
> Elya, Susan Middleton. *Fairy Trails: A Story Told in English and Spanish.*
> Scieszka, Jon. *The Stinky Cheese Man & Other Fairly Stupid Tales.*
> —-. *Summer Reading Is Killing Me!*

✱ Alternate Activity

- Do the lesson above, but subtract a character instead of adding one.
- Have students add themselves as the character in a tale.
- Students will add a character from another fairy tale into a fairy tale of their choice. (For example, what would happen if Jack from "Jack and the Beanstalk" were added to "Beauty and the Beast?")

Setting

Fairy Tale Now

Supports AASL standards   1, 2, 3, 5, 6, 9
Supports NCTE standards   1, 3, 5, 6, 11

One aspect of setting is when the story takes place. This includes the historical period, year, day, and time of day. Students will show their comprehension of setting and use of context clues by changing a fairy tale from olden times to now.

Read a fairy tale aloud to the class. Then ask when the action happens. Most fairy tales directly state they happened long ago. Ask the class for other details that give context clues about the time period. Have students write the fairy tale set in the current time period. Students will read the original tale to a group of younger students and then read their assignments. The tales could also be published in a class or school newsletter. If proper privacy policies are followed, the tales may be posted to the school Web site.

✶ Alternate Activity

- Have students choose and read a fairy tale and then write the tale set in the current time period.
- Choose a different historical period with which students are familiar and ask them to rewrite a fairy tale in that setting.
- Students will read a fairy tale and rewrite it, setting it in the future.
- Have students read a fairy tale, and then have them rewrite it so that day and night action is reversed.

For Sale

Supports AASL standards   1, 2, 3, 5, 6, 9
Supports NCTE standards   3, 4, 5, 6, 11

Place, where the story happens, is the other aspect of setting. This lesson helps students investigate the importance of place, giving them practice with inference and creative critical thinking. Before class, gather enough real estate flyers or ads for each student. Read a fairy tale aloud to students. Ask them to list and describe the places mentioned in the tale. Now have them imagine that they are realtors who are putting one of the fairy tale buildings or lands up for sale. Distribute the flyers and ads and discuss the information given. Then distribute Figure 2.17, For Sale. Students will create their own real estate flyers and present them in small groups or with the entire class when they are finished. Students must be prepared to defend their descriptions based on the text. The flyers may be posted in the library or classroom or be scanned into a computer file.

For Sale

Name _____ Date _____

You are a real estate agent trying to sell a fairy tale building. Complete the form below to create your sales flyer. Draw a picture of the building in the rectangle.

FOR SALE

Address: _____

_____

Short sales description:

_____

Number of bedrooms _____

Number of bathrooms _____

Number of square feet _____

Special features _____

_____

_____

_____

_____

Price _____

Figure 2.17: For Sale

From *Once Upon A Time: Fairy Tales in the Library and Language Arts Classroom for Grades 3-6*, by Jane Heitman. Columbus, OH: Linworth Publishing, Inc. Further reproduction prohibited. Copyright ©2007.

SECTION II: The Lessons 99

Move It

Supports AASL standards   1, 2, 3, 5, 6, 9
Supports NCTE standards   3, 5, 6, 11

In this lesson, students will discover the difference place can make in literature. They will use comprehension and inference skills. Explain to students that part of setting is place, where the story takes place. Then read a fairy tale aloud. After the story, ask students why the place was important. How did it contribute to the story? Next, ask them to think about what the same story would be like if the action took place in their neighborhood. Have students rewrite the fairy tale, moving it to where they live. When they are finished, students will share their tales in small groups or with the entire class.

Theme

My Life Is Like a Fairy Tale

Supports AASL standards   1, 2, 3, 4, 5, 6, 9
Supports NCTE standards   3, 5, 6, 11, 12

This lesson applies students' inference skills and comprehension of theme, a difficult concept for elementary students who may not be abstract thinkers yet. For more information about theme, see Section II, Theme.

Read a fairy tale aloud to the class. Then discuss and identify theme as the author's big idea about life. More than one idea may be correct. Help students use textual evidence to draw their conclusions.

Next, ask students how the themes they have identified apply to their own lives. (This may be a rhetorical question, depending on the dynamics of your class.) Ask students to choose one of the fairy tale themes they have identified, apply that theme to their own lives, and write a contemporary story containing that theme. It may or may not be written in fairy tale style, and it may or may not be fiction. The class will publish a book of these stories in hard copy, in a computer file, or both.

> ## Flip the Theme
>
> **Supports AASL standards** 1, 2, 3, 5, 6, 9
> **Supports NCTE standards** 3, 5, 6, 11
>
> This lesson demonstrates the impact theme makes on a story. Students will exercise comprehension and inference skills. Read a fairy tale aloud to the class. Together, identify story themes based on textual evidence. Ask students to rewrite the fairy tale, but with an opposite theme. For example, if a theme is "the value of friendship," they will rewrite the story with the theme "The fickleness of friendship." Students will share their stories in small groups or with the entire class.

Assessment Suggestions

Some of the previous lessons contain assessment suggestions. Assessments may be formal and informal and include the following:

Self Assessment

Journals are common tools in writing classes. These can be used for self-assessment by asking students to rate their own journal entries or by writing what they have learned. Journals are sometimes used to dialogue in writing between student and educator. Students may track their assignment completion on a chart or in a log and keep all of their work in a folder or portfolio. A folder holds all of a student's work for a unit or time period, while a portfolio has more presentation quality. A portfolio contains a student's work, as well as explanatory notes and narrative by the student about his or her work.

Peer Assessment

Peer assessment is best used as a component of presentations. Students may use the Peer Assessment Template, as described in Section II, Reading, Figure 1.19, Peer Assessment Template.

Library Media Specialist and Teacher Assessment

Observation of students' behavior, group participation, and written work give good informal indicators regarding their progress. Spot-checking students' work allows you to assess without reading every assignment every time. Many education professionals use rubrics or contracts to assess their students. These let students know your expectations in advance and how to reach them. Their marks are never a surprise. A sample rubric follows. For more information about assessments, see Assessment Suggestions, Section II, Reading.

Sample Rubric: Writing, Sequencing

Objectives	Unsatisfactory	Satisfactory	Excellent	Earned Points
Students will use logic to write story in sequence.	**1 point** Student wrote story, but did not apply logical sequence.	**5 points** Student wrote story, using logical sequence most of the time.	**10 points** Student wrote story with each part logically following the next throughout the story.	
Student will use standard English language conventions	**1 point** Student does not use standard English language conventions.	**5 points** Student uses standard English conventions most of the time.	**10 points** Student consistently uses standard English conventions throughout the story.	
			Score	

Figure 2.18: Sample Rubric: Writing, Sequencing

Section III

Speaking and Listening

The following section contains lessons for a variety of types of speaking and some tips for good listening. Some assessment suggestions have been included within the lessons. Other assessment suggestions follow each type of speaking rather than listing them at the end of the section.

Read Aloud

Having students read aloud helps them gain fluency and demonstrates comprehension. Reading aloud helps students connect sight and sound. Practice builds students' confidence.

The Jim Trelease classic, *The Read-Aloud Handbook*, is written for adults, but much of his advice applies to students reading aloud. See a copy (the sixth edition is the newest at the time of this writing) or see the *Trelease-on-Reading* Web site for excerpts of the fifth edition.

Some basic read-aloud tips:
- Choose a book you like.
- Choose a book appropriate for your audience.
- Before you read for an audience, practice.
- Introduce the book briefly, giving the audience a reason to listen.
- Give the title of the book and the names of the author and illustrator.
- If you read a picture book, show the pictures to the audience as you read.
- Read slowly enough so that the audience can experience the story.
- Read with expression.

Before launching a student read-aloud session, model good reading aloud for students and instruct them on the basics. In each case, guide students toward stories that are appropriate for their age, skill, and interest levels. If they will have live audiences, show them stories appropriate for the audience. Talk with students about the stories they have chosen, and help them develop simple introductions to engage their audiences.

Read Aloud to a Pet

Supports AASL standards   1, 4, 5, 9
Supports NCTE standards   1, 2, 3, 4, 11, 12

Asking students to read fairy tales aloud to a pet gives students fluency practice with a warm, non-judgmental audience. Set up a corner where students can read to a stuffed animal, your classroom pet, or a guest animal. Some organizations have assist dogs trained to sit quietly and listen with attention. Schedule students for five- to ten-minute sessions.

Read Aloud Audio Recordings

Supports AASL standards   1, 4, 5, 9
Supports NCTE standards   1, 2, 3, 4, 11, 12

Have students record fairy tales onto cassette tapes to improve their fluency. They will need to practice first so they can read with as few mistakes as possible. Make the tapes available for checkout in the library, taking care to follow copyright laws and guidelines by using only sources in the public domain or obtaining publisher's permission.

Alternatively, students could record their tales on CD-ROM or create an MP3 file of the story and make it downloadable from the school Web site. Your class could also sponsor a "Dial-a-Story" telephone line for the class or community, on which callers hear a pre-recorded fairy tale. Be sure to follow copyright laws and guidelines by using only sources in the public domain or obtaining publisher's permission.

Read Aloud to a Partner

Supports AASL standards   1, 4, 5, 9
Supports NCTE standards   1, 2, 3, 4, 11, 12

Assign or have students choose reading partners, who will work together to improve their fluency and comprehension skills. Have one student read a fairy tale while the other listens; then the other student reads while the other listens. Student partners can be supportive, receptive audiences and help each other with troublesome words. Another way to read as partners is for one student to read one page, and the other student read the next, alternating through the story. Your library may own books that have been designed to be read with two voices, such as Mary Ann Hoberman's *You Read to Me, I'll Read to You*, which would be appropriate for this lesson.

Read Aloud to a Class

Supports AASL standards   1, 4, 5, 9
Supports NCTE standards   1, 2, 3, 4, 11, 12

Have students prepare a fairy tale to read to the class. They should practice with partners, animals, or by themselves at home for fluency and expression, based on comprehension. This activity develops students' presentation skills, such as poise, posture and speech projection and enunciation. The audience practices good listening skills.

▶ Extended Activity

Have students read tales to other groups. Possibilities include other classes, parent or civic groups, public library storytimes, preschools, or senior citizen care facilities.

Assessment Suggestions for Reading Aloud

Many education professionals use rubrics or contracts to assess their students. These let students know your expectations in advance and how to reach them. Figure 3.1, Sample Rubric for Speaking Activities follows. See more information and resources about assessment in Section II, Assessments, Reading.

Sample Rubric for Speaking Activities

Objectives	Unsatisfactory	Satisfactory	Excellent	Earned Points
Students will speak fluently and with appropriate vocal tone.	1 point Student did not speak fluently or use appropriate vocal tone.	5 points Student spoke fluently or used appropriate vocal tone, not both.	10 points Student spoke fluently and used appropriate vocal tone.	
Student will use motions, facial expressions, and eye contact to enhance the listeners' experience.	1 point Student demonstrated one of the three criteria.	5 points Student demonstrated two of the three criteria.	10 points Student demonstrated all three criteria.	
			Score	

Figure 3.1 Sample Rubric for Speaking Activities

Here are some assessment ideas specific to reading aloud:

- Students keep a notebook log, computer file, or word wall of books they read out loud with a self-assessment component.
- Students keep a log of words they do not know, look them up in a dictionary, and write down the definition.
- Librarian and teacher make informal assessment by listening in on students' reading.
- Peers rate each other based on established criteria. Students may use the Peer Assessment Template, as described in Section II, Reading, Figure 1.19, Peer Assessment Template.

Storytelling

Storytelling differs from reading aloud because storytelling is a memorized interpretation of a work. Storytellers may use props, such as stuffed animals, and may have a more dramatic delivery than someone reading aloud. Storytellers begin learning their story from a text or audio source, but they are allowed to change details to make the story their own. They may add local landmarks to give the impression that the story happened in the audience's town, for example. They may create a refrain or have some repeated action they invite the audience to say or do. They may lengthen or shorten the original story, depending on the audience. Storytelling, even more than reading aloud, develops rapport between audience and storyteller and among the audience.

If possible, bring a storyteller to your school, so students can experience being told a story without book in hand. The storyteller must help students create visuals in their imaginations. Storytellers may be professionals or volunteers. Your area may have a storytelling group, such as Spellbinders, that trains volunteers to tell stories in schools. The National Storytelling Network offers support to professional and amateur storytellers and hosts storytelling events. Its "How to Become a Storyteller" page gives tips for beginners. Though aimed at adults, the same basic tips apply.

> For more information, see:
> *National Storytelling Network* <www.storynet.org/>
> *Spellbinders* <www.spellbinders.org/>
> Weissman, Annie. *Do Tell! Storytelling for You and Your Students*. Worthington, OH: Linworth, 2002.

In selecting a story to tell, students will access and read a range of stories and apply literacy strategies. Students will choose or adapt a story appropriate for themselves and for a particular audience. They will use expression during the telling. Since many stories, especially fairy tales, are from a variety of cultures, students will develop awareness for the culture and its language. Storytelling occurs in community, creating a bond among the teller and the listeners.

Storytelling Practice

Supports AASL standards   1, 4, 5, 9
Supports NCTE standards   1, 2, 3, 4, 9, 11, 12

Students will apply comprehension, critical thinking, and fluency in storytelling. Storytelling requires even more practice than reading aloud. Help your students find fairy tales they like. They can learn the story by reading it to animals and partners, as described in the previous Read Aloud section. Then have them practice telling the story in front of the class or a smaller group, with the audience critiquing the storyteller using Figure 3.2 Storytelling Critique Sheet.

Storytelling Critique Sheet

Name _____ Date _____

Storyteller _____

Title of Story _____

_____

For each statement, circle the appropriate number describing how well the storyteller presented the story. Three is best, and one is least.

The storyteller knew the story well.	1	2	3
The storyteller told the story smoothly.	1	2	3
The storyteller looked at the audience.	1	2	3
The storyteller used appropriate motions.	1	2	3
The storyteller helped me see the story in my mind.	1	2	3
The story was appropriate for the speaker and the audience.	1	2	3

Figure 3.2: Storytelling Critique Sheet

From *Once Upon A Time: Fairy Tales in the Library and Language Arts Classroom for Grades 3-6*, by Jane Heitman. Columbus, OH: Linworth Publishing, Inc. Further reproduction prohibited. Copyright ©2007.

Ready, Set, Tell

Supports AASL standards   1, 4, 5, 9
Supports NCTE standards   1, 2, 3, 4, 9, 11, 12

Students will practice their comprehension, critical thinking, and fluency skills in this activity. After practicing and refining, send student storytellers into other classrooms, to civic groups, and other appropriate venues.

Storytelling Festival

Supports AASL standards   1, 4, 5, 9
Supports NCTE standards   1, 2, 3, 4, 9, 11, 12

Help students hone their comprehension, critical thinking, fluency, and presentation skills by hosting a storytelling festival. A festival can be as small and simple as setting aside one class period in the library or classroom for one class. It can be as elaborate as an assembly involving the entire school with outside guests or an event for the entire community.

A simple festival involves the following:

- Get permission from the proper administrators.
- Set a date, place, and time.
- Enlist help from parents, school volunteers, and other teachers.
- Prepare student storytellers. Be sure they have plenty of practice before festival day.
- Send invitations to any outside guests (students' families, for example).
- Decide the students' speaking order, varying story plots and tones and student ability levels.
- Create a printed program. Include a bibliography of books on which the storytelling is based. If possible, have the books available to check out.
- Provide refreshments (optional).
- Arrange the room in the way you want it.
- Designate an emcee or introduce each storyteller yourself.
- Applaud each story and thank everyone for participating at the end.

Assessment Suggestions for Storytelling

Using rubrics lets students know your expectations in advance, and helps students work toward reaching them. See Figure 3.1, Sample Rubric for Speaking Activities or Section II, Reading, Assessments for rubric samples and resources.

Here are some assessment suggestions specific to storytelling:

- Use informal feedback from listeners. Encourage students to tell why they liked or did not like a story or portion of a story.
- Students may keep a self-assessment journal tracking their progress. The self-assessment should contain these parts: What I Did Well, What I Did Less Well, and How I Can Improve.
- Students complete Figure 3.2, Storytelling Critique Sheet.

Choral Reading

Choral reading is reading as a group for improved fluency and comprehension and for the satisfaction and enjoyment of the group. It is a simple, read vocal dramatization. (Script memorization is allowed, but not required.) Choral reading involves the whole class, but it can feature parts, too. Prepared scripts are available at sources such as *Scripts for Schools Choral Reading* online (www.scriptsforschools.com/29.html), but deciding parts as a class helps students analyze the fairy tale, increasing comprehension.

Read It Together

Supports AASL standards   1, 2, 3, 5, 6, 9
Supports NCTE standards   1, 2, 3, 4, 6, 8, 11, 12

The benefits of reading aloud as a group reinforce the power of language and the variety of ways it can be used. Fluency, critical thinking, expression, and comprehension skills are all taught through choral reading.

Choose a script or write your own. Decide together what should be spoken loudly or softly, quickly or slowly, high or low. Which are the girls' parts; which are the boys'? Project the tale you've chosen double-spaced on an overhead transparency or computer. Then write or type in parts beside the words. An example of choral reading directions follows:

Hansel and Gretel

All: Once upon a time

Girls: There dwelt near a large wood

Boys: A poor woodcutter

Girls: With his wife and two children by his former marriage,

Boys: A little boy called Hansel

Girls: And a girl named Gretel.

Boys: He had little enough to break or bite, and once, when there was a great famine in the land, he could not procure even his daily bread.

Girls: And as he lay thinking in his bed one evening, rolling about for trouble, he sighed, and said to his wife

Boy 1: What will become of us? How can we feed our children when we have no more than we can eat ourselves?

Girl 1: Know then my husband

Boys: Answered she,

Girl 1: We will lead them away quite early in the morning into the thickest part of the wood....

(Opie 312)

> Practice the tale together until it flows with the vocal effects you desire. Then perform the piece for another class or special event. If you have copyright permission or have used tales in the public domain, record the reading and keep the recording in the library. You could also create a computer audio file to download from the school Web site.

Assessment Suggestions for Choral Reading

Since choral reading is intended for the purpose of the audience, group assessment, led by the library media specialist or teacher, is an appropriate tool. Ask students to rate their performance on the following factors:

- Speakers were on cue.
- All speakers participated enthusiastically.
- Speakers used an appropriate tone.
- Speakers followed directions.

Readers Theater

A more formal dramatization method is Readers Theater (RT). (You will also see "Reader's Theater," "Readers' Theater," and "Theatre" rather than "Theater.") RT is reading aloud dramatically to communicate a story. While choral reading's intent is for the pleasure of the participant, RT is designed for an audience.

As with choral reading, your arrangements can be as simple or elaborate as time, budget, and imagination allow. While memorizing the script is allowed, holding scripts and reading is acceptable and more practical. Simple costuming, such as hats or masks to depict different characters, is often used. Simple set pieces, such as tables or stools, can suggest trees, houses, and other locales. RT usually has more solo lines than choral reading.

Reading as Play

Supports AASL standards 1, 2, 3, 5, 6, 9
Supports NCTE standards 1, 2, 3, 4, 6, 8, 11, 12

Readers theater develops fluency, comprehension, and reading with expression. Its performance aspect helps students gain poise and engages their creativity and critical thinking.

Choose a script or write your own.

Commercial scripts are available from a variety of sources, including:

Gustafson, Chris. *Acting Cool! Using Reader's Theatre to Teach Language Arts and Social Studies in Your Classroom.* Worthington, OH: Linworth, 2003.

—-. *Acting Out: Reader's Theatre Across the Curriculum.* Worthington, OH: Linworth, 2002.

Scripts for Schools. 02 June 2007 <www.scriptsforschools.com>.

Shepard, Aaron. *Aaron Shepard's RT Page.* 02 June 2007 <www.aaronshep.com/rt/index.html>.

Creating your own scripts takes some time and effort but also allows you to customize your production for your students and audience. To write your own script, choose a traditional fairy tale or a version of a favorite fairy tale. Consider how many strong readers you have and give them the main parts. The rest of the class can participate as "the chorus." Your class can also write their own RT scripts, once they've seen one. Here's an example:

Characters: Narrator - glasses, carrying large book
Woodcutter - lumberjack cap
Woodcutter's wife - kerchief on head
Hansel - baseball cap
Gretel - apron
Witch - witch hat
Chorus - everyone else

Set: Two chairs on one side of stage, three chairs on the other, coat rack in between to act as woods.

Chorus: Once upon a time there dwelt near a large wood
Woodcutter: A poor woodcutter
Woodcutter's wife: his wife
Hansel and Gretel: and two children by his former marriage,
Hansel: a little boy called Hansel
Gretel: and a girl named Gretel.
Narrator: He had little enough to break or bite, and once, when there was a great famine in the land, he could not procure even his daily bread; and as he lay thinking in his bed one evening, rolling about for trouble, he sighed
Woodcutter: (Sighs. Turns to wife.) What will become of us? How can we feed our children when we have no more than we can eat ourselves?
Woodcutter's wife: Know then, my husband, we will lead them away quite early in the morning into the thickest part of the wood....
(Opie 312)

Assessment Suggestions for Readers Theater

Audience applause may be the most rewarding assessment for readers theater, but a more objective assessment may be desired. Library media specialists and teachers, audience members, and performers may rate performances on these criteria:

- Performer's use of appropriate posture for the role
- Performer's use of appropriate tone for the role
- Performer is on cue
- Performer speaks convincingly as the character

Puppet Theater

Harness students' enjoyment of producing and watching puppet theater shows to help improve their comprehension, critical thinking, fluency, and presentation skills. Many books contain puppet theater scripts, theater construction instructions, and puppet patterns. Some of these contain adaptations of fairy tales. Alternatively, you and your students can write your own puppet theater scripts. You may like to collaborate with drama and art teachers or enlist the aid of a volunteer.

Large puppet theaters can be made from large cardboard boxes, such as appliance boxes. Small puppet theaters can be made from shoeboxes. A large desk in the front of the room can serve as a no-frills puppet theater.

Puppets can be made from cut out cardstock patterns, paper bags, gloves, stuffed animals, or other materials.

Puppet Theater Resources

Bair, Linda and Jill Andrews. *Fee Fi Fo Fum: Puppets & Other Folktale Fun*. Ft. Atkinson, WI: Upstart, 2005.

Carreiro, Carolyn. *Make Your Own Puppets & Puppet Theaters*. Nashville, TN: Williamson, 2005.

Frey, Yvonne Amar. *One-Person Puppetry Streamlined and Simplified: With 38 Folktale Scripts*. Chicago: American Library Association, 2004.

Kennedy, John E. *Puppet Mania: The World's Most Incredible Puppet Making Book Ever*. Cincinnati, OH: North Light, 2004.

Latshaw, George. *The Complete Book of Puppetry*. Mineola, NY: Dover, 2000.

Lohnes, Marilyn. *Fractured Fairy Tales: Puppet Plays & Patterns*. Ft. Atkinson, WI: Upstart, 2002.

Mahlmann, Lewis. *Plays for Young Puppeteers: 25 Puppet Plays for Easy Performance*. Boston: Plays, Inc., 1993.

Minkel, Walter. *How to Do "The Three Bears" with Two Hands: Performing with Puppets*. Chicago: American Library Association, 1999.

Puppet Play

Supports AASL standards   1, 2, 3, 4,
Supports NCTE standards   1, 2, 3, 4, 5, 6, 8, 11, 12

Students will apply comprehension, critical thinking, and fluency skills by producing a puppet theater show. They will learn to select appropriate scripts (or write their own), follow instructions in the creation of the theater and puppets, exercise creativity, and contribute to the learning community.

Before launching your pre-production activities, get permission from the proper administrators. Puppet theater can be produced and performed by one or two students or by a group. Decide on the group size and whether you want several groups developing productions simultaneously. Determine who the audience will be. The play should be performed for the class, but could also be given for younger grades, a school assembly, or parent and civic groups. Next, help the group

- Choose or write a script
- Assign parts and production responsibilities
- Choose puppet style
- Choose theater style
- Create puppets
- Create theater
- Publicize the production to your intended audience
- Rehearse

The day of the production, be sure the audience has chairs and the theater's set pieces and puppets are in place. Designate an emcee or act as the emcee, welcoming the audience and introducing the play. Lead loud applause at the end, and thank the audience for coming.

Following the production, engage students in a discussion to assess their efforts. You may do a more formal evaluation later.

Drama

The Play's the Thing

Supports AASL standards 1, 2, 3, 5, 7, 9
Supports NCTE standards 1, 2, 3, 4, 5, 6, 11, 12

In play production, students develop comprehension, critical thinking, fluency, and presentation skills. Working in small groups, students will choose a fairy tale or an adaptation of a fairy tale and rewrite it in script form. They will determine necessary set, prop, and costume pieces, though simplicity is encouraged. After allowing time for rehearsal, each group will perform its play for the class. They may also perform for other classes or community venues. Developing a performance reinforces appropriate use of language, demonstrates comprehension, encourages creativity, and builds poise and confidence.

✱ Alternate Activity

Rather than writing original scripts, purchase one from the many companies who publish scripts for school use.

Script Sources

Baker's Plays <www.bakersplays.com>
Contemporary Drama Service <www.contemporarydrama.com>
Dramatic Publishing <www.dramaticpublishing.com>
Pioneer Drama Service, Inc. <www.pioneerdrama.com>
Playscripts, Inc. <www.playscripts.com>
Samuel French, Inc. <www.samuelfrench.com>

Assessment Suggestions for Drama

Every student drama performance deserves hearty applause for the effort alone. Dramas may be rated more formally on the following traits:

- Actors' preparedness
- Actors' speech volume
- Actors speak and act so as to convey characters
- Actors convey the appropriate mood

   Peer assessments or educator assessments may be made using rubrics, such as Figure 3.1, Sample Rubric for Speaking Activities. For more information about rubrics and assessments, see Section II, Reading, Assessments.

Fairy Tale Talk Show

Supports AASL standards   1, 2, 5, 8, 9
Supports NCTE standards   1, 2, 3, 4, 5, 6, 8, 11, 12

Performing a talk show allows students the opportunity to use critical thinking and inference to analyze both characters and tales. It develops their comprehension, fluency, and presentation skills, yet lets them participate as part of a learning community. They will read a variety of tales, including those from other cultures, and apply their creativity while acting in character.

If students have not seen a talk show, explain the premise. The emcee sits behind a desk and introduces one person at a time. The person sits in a chair next to the desk and answers the emcee's questions. When the second person is introduced the first person moves down a chair.

Divide the class into groups of five students. Ask each group to choose a fairy tale. Four group members will choose to be a character from their chosen tale, and the fifth member will be the emcee. All group members will read several versions of their chosen tale, paying particular attention to their character. Distribute Figure 3.3, Character Qualities Planning Template, to guide each student. The emcee will look for an overview of each character and create three or four questions appropriate for each. The questions should be open-ended, without "yes" or "no" answers. Distribute Figure 3.4, Emcee Planning Template, to guide emcees. (If necessary, you or another adult could be the emcee.) Explain to the students who will be characters that the questions they are asked will probably not have direct answers from the story. They will need to use inference skills to answer as the character would. You may like students to improvise their talk show (as a real talk show does), or you may allow emcees to give characters their questions in advance so they have time to think about their answers.

The day of the talk show performances, in the front of the room, set up a desk with a chair behind it and four chairs in a row beside it. The emcee takes the chair at the desk and one by one introduces the talk show guests and chats with them. The rest of the class acts as the audience.

After each group's talk show, discuss with the class how effective and accurate each character was. Distribute Figure 3.5, Talk Show Assessment Template, to the class to complete after the discussion. Continue until all the groups have put on their talk shows.

Character Qualities Planning Template

Name _____ Date _____

Complete the blanks to give information about my character.

My character name is _____. My age is _____.

I look like _____

I live _____

My family members are _____
_____

I spend my time _____

The best thing that ever happened to me is _____
_____

The worst thing that ever happened to me is _____
_____

A turning point in my life was _____
_____

Three words that describe my personality are _____
_____

What I really wanted from life is _____
_____

I reached my goal (or did not reach my goal) by doing this _____
_____

The next thing I want to do is _____

Figure 3.3 Character Qualities Planning Template

From *Once Upon A Time: Fairy Tales in the Library and Language Arts Classroom for Grades 3-6*, by Jane Heitman. Columbus, OH: Linworth Publishing, Inc. Further reproduction prohibited. Copyright ©2007.

Emcee Planning Template

A talk show should be like two people talking. You start the program and guide it along. Guests will answer your comments and questions. They may lead you in surprising directions. Go ahead and follow up. You do not have to follow your list of questions. However, please stay within the general action of the character's story. If the character goes outside the action of the story, bring him or her back with an appropriate question. Here are some ideas of what to say. Add your own.

Character 1

- Give character name and tell something interesting about the character.
- Ask how he or she felt about that interesting thing.
- Ask how he or she reached his goal (or why he or she did not, if he or she did not).
- Ask how his or her background helped or slowed down reaching the goal.

Other:_____

Character 2

- Give character name and tell why this character is famous.
- Ask what is good and what is bad about being famous.
- Ask how friends and family treat the character differently since he or she became famous.
- Ask how the character will use his or her fame.

Other:_____

Character 3

- Give character name and tell something about the character's background.
- Ask how the bad things in the character's past helped him or her become the character he or she is today.
- Ask what character qualities have been most important to him or her.
- Ask who has had the greatest effect on the character and why.

Other:_____

Character 4

- Give character name and tell something about the character's homeland.
- Ask what he or she likes best about his or her homeland.
- Ask what he or she likes least about his or her homeland.
- Ask what effect the character's homeland has had on his or her life.

Other:_____

Figure 3.4: Emcee Planning Template

From *Once Upon A Time: Fairy Tales in the Library and Language Arts Classroom for Grades 3-6*, by Jane Heitman. Columbus, OH: Linworth Publishing, Inc. Further reproduction prohibited. Copyright ©2007.

Talk Show Assessment Template

Name _____ Date _____

Character I am assessing _____

Real Name _____

For each statement, circle the appropriate number describing how well this student acted his or her part. Three is best, and one is least.

This student knew basic facts about the character.	1	2	3
This student knew basic facts about the character's story.	1	2	3
This student projected beyond the story in appropriate ways.	1	2	3
This student spoke smoothly, with appropriate tone.	1	2	3
This student used motions and posture as the character would.	1	2	3

Figure 3.5: Talk Show Assessment Template

From *Once Upon A Time: Fairy Tales in the Library and Language Arts Classroom for Grades 3-6*, by Jane Heitman. Columbus, OH: Linworth Publishing, Inc. Further reproduction prohibited. Copyright ©2007.

Guilty or Not Guilty?

Supports AASL standards   1, 2, 3, 6, 7, 8, 9
Supports NCTE standards   4, 7, 11

Holding a mock trial for a fairy tale character will develop students' ability to access and evaluate information, use information accurately and creatively, generate knowledge, and participate in a democratic function as part of a community. Students will apply comprehension, critical thinking, and inference skills. They will determine cause and effect and articulate the main action.

Choose a fairy tale character and charge him or her with a crime. Here are some suggestions:

Character	*Charge*
Jack	Theft
Cinderella's stepmother	Child abuse
Snow White	Trespassing
Hansel & Gretel's father	Child abandonment
The Witch in Hansel & Gretel	Attempted murder
The Maiden in Rumpelstiltskin	Breach of Contract

You can make these crimes against the state, where the prosecutor represents "the people," or you can make these crimes specifically against another character. For example, in "Snow White v. the Seven Dwarfs," Snow White could be charged with trespassing against the dwarfs.

Collaborate with your social sciences teacher to teach students basic legal procedures and courtroom protocol. If possible, invite a legal expert to speak to the class about preparing a case. If a high school in your district sponsors a mock trial team, ask the advisor if it can assist your class. The 19th Circuit Court of Lake & McHenry Counties, Illinois, offers basic instructions on their Web page, "Guide to Conducting Mock Trials." Mock trial scripts are available for purchase from the American Bar Association (ABA), Public Education Division. The ABA Web page, "Mock Trials," also offers a complete lesson plan with instructions for conducting a mock trial.

Choose students to act as judge (you may choose an adult for this role), defendant (the character charged), attorneys for the defense and the plaintiff, bailiff, witnesses for the defense and the plaintiff, and jury. A court reporter is optional. If the class is large, each attorney may have a team of lawyers.

Each student must study his or her character and his or her role in the trial. You and the adults with whom you collaborate should work closely with students during the preparation phase. The lawyers must prepare their cases and decide which witnesses to call to the stand. They must decide which questions to ask their witnesses and anticipate the other side's arguments. They must be able to think quickly and logically as they cross-examine witnesses for the opposing side. Witnesses must be characters in the story and answer questions as they think the characters would.

The room where the trial takes place will need a large desk for the judge, a chair next to the desk for the witness being questioned, a row of chairs to the side for the jury, and two tables with chairs facing the judge's desk for the attorneys. The jury needs a separate area to conduct their deliberations.

The order of events in a mock trial is listed below.

- The jury, attorneys, their clients, and the witnesses are all seated.
- The bailiff declares the court in session, "the Honorable Judge (name) presiding," and asks all to rise.
- The judge enters and asks each attorney to make an opening statement.
- After opening statements, the plaintiff's attorney calls witnesses to the stand.
- Each witness answers the attorney's questions.
- The opposing attorney cross-examines (asks questions of) the witness.
- This continues until all of the plaintiff's witnesses are questioned.
- The opposing attorney's witnesses are called, questioned, and cross-examined.
- Each attorney gives closing remarks.
- The jury goes to a separate area to deliberate. Their decision must be unanimous.
- When the jury has reached a verdict, they return to the courtroom.
- They hand their written verdict to the bailiff.
- The bailiff reads the verdict aloud.
- Usually, sentencing is a separate procedure. In this mock trial, the judge will declare the sentence if the verdict is guilty.

✻ Alternate Activity

Rather than having students improvise their courtroom experience, work together as a class to discuss the parts and create a script for students to follow as they enact the trial.

⮕ Extended Activity

Videotape the trial and play it so students can assess their performances. Ask them what they would do differently with their characters, if anything. Ask how well each student represented his or her character.

Listening

Reason would dictate that speakers need listeners, and students may need training in appropriate listening behavior for a variety of activities. Neither AASL nor NCTE standards mentions listening. NCTE standard 11, about participating in literacy communities, is as close as these national standards get. Some states and school districts do have a listening component to their standards.

Your library or classroom may already have a set of listening rules or guidelines. If not, work with your classes to create a list and post it where students can see it during activities. Reinforce these guidelines and any special audience instructions before each event.

A good introduction can create a better audience by asking the audience to listen for something in particular, or by asking them to clap or raise their hands when they hear a certain word. A short introduction related to the plot creates audience interest and generates suspense and excitement. This helps make students ready to listen.

My local public library staff introduces puppet shows by telling children to remain seated so everyone can see, to shout out answers to questions the puppets ask them, and not to pick up anything that comes flying out of the puppet theater. The children know what to do when these things occur and feel safe in their participatory behavior.

Audiences listening to stories read aloud or told should be quiet unless the reader or teller asks the audience to say something. However, laughing out loud at funny parts, groaning at silly parts, and gasping at scary parts are fine ways of engaging in the story. Audiences should direct their attention to the story reader or teller throughout the story and sit still unless the speaker asks the audience to move. Applause at the end is always appropriate. An audience's appropriate engagement with the story encourages the speaker to do his or her best.

Guidelines for readers theater and puppet theater are similar, but here students should be even more engaged visually. The audience should respond to the costume, props, and set effects, as well as the theatrical vocalization of the story. Readers theater and puppet theater offer a more complete experience than basic read-alouds.

Guidelines for choral reading differ because choral reading is intended for participants, not audiences. As a participant in choral reading, students must listen to the text and recognize cues for their parts. They must listen to their own voices and modulate them for proper dynamics and tone. Their careful listening will lead to a more effective reading and more satisfying experience.

Assessment Suggestions for Listening

- Peers may rate each other using Figure 3.6, Listening Peer Assessment Template.
- The speaker may rate the audience. The speaker may use Figure 3.6, Listening Peer Assessment Template.
- Library media specialist and teacher may assess, using criteria similar to that in Figure 3.6, Listening Peer Assessment Template.

Listening Peer Assessment Template

Name _____ Date _____

Assignment _____

For each statement, circle the appropriate number describing how well your group listened. Three is best, and one is least.

My group faced the speaker the entire time.   1   2   3

My group listened quietly to the speaker the entire time.   1   2   3

My group helped the speaker by nodding and reacting   1   2   3
appropriately.

Complete this sentence: My group could be better listeners by

_____

_____ .

Overall, I rate my group   1   2   3

Figure 3.6: Listening Peer Assessment Template

From *Once Upon A Time: Fairy Tales in the Library and Language Arts Classroom for Grades 3-6*, by Jane Heitman. Columbus, OH: Linworth Publishing, Inc. Further reproduction prohibited. Copyright ©2007.

Works Cited

Books

Aarne, Antti. *The Types of the Folktale, a Classification and Bibliography*. Helsinki, Finland: Suomalainen Tiedeakatemia, 1961.

American Association of School Librarians, and Association for Educational Communications and Technology. *Information Power: Building Partnerships for Learning*. Chicago: American Library Assn., 1998.

Bair, Linda, and Jill Andrews. *Fee Fi Fo Fum: Puppets & Other Folktale Fun*. Ft. Atkinson, WI: Upstart, 2005.

Bettelheim, Bruno. *Uses of Enchantment*. New York: Knopf, 1977.

Buzzeo, Toni. *Collaborating to Meet Standards: Teacher/Librarian Partnerships for K-6*. Worthington, OH: Linworth, 2002.

Carreiro, Carolyn. *Make Your Own Puppets & Puppet Theaters*. Nashville, TN: Williamson, 2005.

Child, Lauren. *Who's Afraid of the Big Bad Book*. New York: Hyperion, 2003.

Ellis, John M. *One Fairy Story Too Many: The Brothers Grimm and Their Tales*. Chicago: U of Chicago P, 1983.

Elya, Susan Middleton. *Fairy Trails: A Story Told in English and Spanish*. New York: Bloomsbury, 2005.

Fiderer, Adele. *40 Rubrics & Checklists to Assess Reading and Writing: Time-Saving Reproducible Forms and Great Strategies for Meaningful Assessment*. New York: Scholastic, 1999.

Frey, Yvonne Amar. *One-person Puppetry Streamlined and Simplified: With 38 Folktale Scripts*. Chicago: American Library Association, 2004.

Glandon, Shan. *Integrating Technology: Effective Tools for Collaboration*. Worthington, OH: Linworth, 2002.

Griswold, Jerry. *The Meanings of "Beauty and the Beast": A Handbook*. Peterborough, Ont.: Broadview, 2004.

Groeber, Joan F. *Designing Rubrics for Reading and Language Arts*. Arlington Heights, IL: SkyLight, 2003.

Gustafson, Chris. *Acting Cool! Using Reader's Theatre to Teach Language Arts and Social Studies in Your Classroom*. Worthington, OH: Linworth, 2003.

—. *Acting Out: Reader's Theatre Across the Curriculum*. Worthington, OH: Linworth, 2002.

Heitman, Jane. *Rhymes and Reasons: Using Poetry to Foster Literacy*. Worthington, OH: Linworth, 2003.

Hoberman, Mary Ann. *You Read to Me, I'll Read to You*. New York: Little, 2004.

Hollenbeck, Kathleen M. *Teaching with Cinderella Stories from Around the World*. New York: Scholastic, 2003.

Kennedy, John E. *Puppet Mania: The World's Most Incredible Puppet Making Book Ever.* Cincinnati, OH: North Light, 2004.

Kready, Laura F. *A Study of Fairy Tales.* Boston: Houghton, 1916.

Latshaw, George. *The Complete Book of Puppetry.* Mineola, NY: Dover, 2000.

Lohnes, Marilyn. *Fractured Fairy Tales: Puppet Plays & Patterns.* Ft. Atkinson, WI: Upstart, 2002.

Lüthi, Max. *The Fairytale as Art Form and Portrait of Man.* Bloomington: Indiana UP, 1984.

—. *Once Upon a Time: On the Nature of Fairy Tales.* Bloomington: Indiana UP, 1976, c 1970.

Mahlmann, Lewis. *Plays for Young Puppeteers: 25 Puppet Plays for Easy Performance.* Boston: Plays, Inc., 1993.

McGlathery, James M. *Grimms' Fairy Tales: A History of Criticism on a Popular Classic.* Columbia, SC: Camden, 1993.

Minkel, Walter. *How to Do "The Three Bears" with Two Hands: Performing with Puppets.* Chicago: American Library Assn., 1999.

Nichols, Beverly, et al. *Managing Curriculum and Assessment: A Practitioner's Guide.* Worthington, OH: Linworth, 2006.

Opie, Iona, and Peter Opie. *The Classic Fairy Tales.* New York: Oxford UP, 1974.

Scieszka, Jon. *The Stinky Cheese Man & Other Fairly Stupid Tales.* New York: Viking, 2002.

—. *Summer Reading Is Killing Me!* New York: Viking, 1998.

—. *The True Story of the 3 Little Pigs by A. Wolf.* New York: Viking, 1989.

Simpson, Carol. *Copyright Catechism: Practical Answers to Real Copyright Questions from Educators.* Worthington, OH: Linworth, 2005.

—. *Copyright for Schools: A Practical Guide.* 4th ed. Worthington, OH: Linworth, 2005.

—. *Copyright Responsibilities for Educators...Quick Pocket Guide.* Worthington, OH: Linworth, 2005.

Sullivan, Mary. *75 Language Arts Assessment Tools.* New York: Scholastic, 2003.

Tatar, Maria. *The Hard Facts of the Grimms' Fairy Tales.* Princeton, N.J.: Princeton UP, 1987.

Tompkins, Gail E. *Teaching Writing: Balancing Process and Product.* 4th ed. Upper Saddle River, NJ: Prentice, 2003.

Trelease, Jim. *The Read-Aloud Handbook.* 6th ed. New York: Penguin, 2006.

Vande Velde, Vivian. *Tales from the Brothers Grimm and the Sisters Weird.* Orlando, FL: Magic Carpet, 2005.

Weissman, Annie. *Do Tell! Storytelling for You and Your Students.* Worthington, OH: Linworth, 2002.

Yolen, Jane. *Fairy Tale Feasts: A Literary Cookbook for Young Readers and Eaters.* Recipes by Heidi E.Y. Stemple. Northampton, MA: Crocodile, 2006.

Young, Sue. *Scholastic Guides: Writing with Style.* New York: Scholastic, 1999.

Zipes, Jack. *Breaking the Magic Spell: Radical Theories of Folk and Fairy Tales.* Austin: U of Texas P, 1979.

—. *When Dreams Came True: Classical Fairy Tales and Their Tradition.* New York: Routledge, 1999.

Web Sites

American Association of School Librarians, and Association for Educational Communications and Technology. *Information Literacy Standards for Student Learning*. 1998. American Library Assn. 02 June 2007 <www.ala.org/ala/aasl/aasl-proftools/informationpower/InformationLiteracyStandards_final.pdf>.

Ashliman, D. L. *Rapunzel*. 22 Jun. 2006. 02 June 2007 <www.pitt.edu/~dash/grimm012a.html>.

Baker's Plays. 02 June 2007. <www.bakersplays.com>.

"Choral Speaking Scripts Catalog." *Scripts for Schools*. 02 June 2007 <www.scriptsforschools.com/29.html>.

Contemporary Drama Service. 02 June 2007 <www.contemporarydrama.com>.

Dramatic Publishing. 20 Sept. 2006. 02 June 2007 <www.dramaticpublishing.com>.

"Fractured Fairy Tales & Fables with Jon Scieszka." *Scholastic*. 02 June 2007 <http://teacher.scholastic.com/writewit/mff/fractured_fairy.htm>.

"Guide to Conducting Mock Trials." *Nineteenth Judicial Circuit Court of Lake County, Illinois*. 02 June 2007 <www.19thcircuitcourt.state.il.us/bkshelf/resource/mt_conduct.htm>.

Hastings, Waller. *Defining the Fairy Tale*. Aberdeen, SD: Northern State U. 15 June 2003. 02 June 2007 <www.northern.edu/hastingsw/ftdefine.htm>.

Heiner, Heidi Anne. "History of Beauty and the Beast." *SurLaLune Fairy Tales*. 3 Nov. 2003. 02 June 2007 <www.surlalunefairytales.com/beautybeast/history.html>.

—. "History of Cinderella." *SurLaLune Fairy Tales*. 1 Dec. 2004. 02 June 2007 <www.surlalunefairytales.com/cinderella/history.html>.

—. "History of Hansel and Gretel." *SurLaLune Fairy Tales*. 1 Dec. 2002. 02 June 2007 <www.surlalunefairytales.com/hanselgretel/history.html>.

—. "History of Jack and the Beanstalk." *SurLaLune Fairy Tales*. 18 Dec. 2003. 02 June 2007 <www.surlalunefairytales.com/jackbeanstalk/history.html>.

—. "History of Rapunzel." *SurLaLune Fairy Tales*. 12 Nov. 2002. 02 June 2007 <www.surlalunefairytales.com/rapunzel/history.html>.

—. "History of Rumpelstiltskin" *SurLaLune Fairy Tales*. 11 Nov. 2002. 02 June 2007 <www.surlalunefairytales.com/rumpelstiltskin/history.html>.

—. "History of Sleeping Beauty." *SurLaLune Fairy Tales*. 6 Nov. 2002. 02 June 2007 <www.surlalunefairytales.com/sleepingbeauty/history.html>.

—. "History of Snow White and the Seven Dwarfs." *SurLaLune Fairy Tales*. 12 Nov. 2002. 02 June 2007 <www.surlalunefairytales.com/sevendwarfs/history.html>.

—. "What Is a Fairy Tale?" *SurLaLune Fairy Tales*. 1 Nov. 2002. 02 June 2007 <www.surlalunefairytales.com/introduction/ftdefinition.html>.

"How to Become a Storyteller." *National Storytelling Network*. 02 June 2007 <www.storynet.org/Resources/KnowledgeBank/howtobecomeastoryteller.html>.

"How to Make an Authentic Medieval Coat of Arms." *Owl & Mouse Educational Software*. 02 June 2007 <www.yourchildlearns.com/her_act.htm>.

Mertz, Gayle. "Grades 4-6: Due Process Freedoms, Yertle the Turtle Mock Trial." *Law Day—May 1*. American Bar Assn. 02 June 2007 <www.abanet.org/publiced/law-day/schools/lessons/46_dueprocess_yertle.html>.

"Mock Trials." American Bar Assn. Public Education Div. 02 June 2007 <www.abanet.org/publiced/mocktrials.html#k6>.

Monster. 02 June 2007 <www.monster.com>.

Pioneer Drama Service, Inc. 02 June 2007 <www.pioneerdrama.com>.

Playscripts, Inc. 02 June 2007 <www.playscripts.com>.

Recipes.com. 02 June 2007 <www.recipes.com>.

Samuel French, Inc. 02 June 2007 <www.samuelfrench.com>.

Schrock, Kathleen. "Teacher Helpers: Assessment & Rubric Information." *Kathy Schrock's Guide for Educators*. Discovery Education. 02 June 2007 <http://school.discovery.com/schrockguide/assess.html>.

Scripts for Schools. 02 June 2007 <www.scriptsforschools.com>.

Shepard, Aaron. *Author Online!* 02 June 2007 <www.aaronshep.com/>.

—-. *Aaron Shepard's RT Page*. 02 June 2007 <www.aaronshep.com/rt/index.html>.

Spellbinders. 02 June 2007 <www.spellbinders.org/>.

"Standards for the English Language Arts." *National Council of Teachers of English*. 02 June 2007 <www.ncte.org/about/over/standards/110846.htm>.

Trelease, Jim. "Excerpted from Jim Trelease's The Read-Aloud Handbook." *Trelease-on-Reading.com*. 02 June 2007 <www.trelease-on-reading.com/rah_intro_p1.html>.

Vandergrift, Kay E. *Snow White*. 02 June 2007 <www.scils.rutgers.edu/~kvander/snowwhite.html>.

Index

A

Aarne, Antti, 2, 3, 11, 14, 17, 19, 21, 24, 28, 124
Aaron Shepard's RT Page, 112, 127
AASL, xi, xv, xvi, 126
Abadeha: The Philippine Cinderella, 4
Accardo, Anthony, 24
access and evaluate information, 120
acrostic poem, 88
Acting Cool! Using Reader's Theatre to Teach Language Arts and Social Studies in Your Classroom, 112, 124
Acting Out: Reader's Theatre Across the Curriculum, 112, 124
Adelita: A Mexican Cinderella Story, 5
Aiken, Joan, 20
American Bar Association (ABA), Public Education Division, 120, 127
American Library Association, xi, xiv
analyze characters and tales, 51, 95, 110, 116
Andrews, Jill, 113, 124
articulate, 65, 120
Ashliman, D.L., 10, 11, 126
assess, 69, 101, 114, 121
Assessment, 51, 61-65, 72, 81, 101-102, 106, 109, 111, 113, 115, 119, 122, 123
AT Index, 2, 3, 10, 14, 16, 19, 21, 23, 28
August, Louise, 6
Author Online!, 127

B

B.A.T., 24
Baca, Ana, 24
Bair, Linda, 113, 124
Baker's Plays, 115, 126
Barrett, Angela, 20
Basile, 10, 14, 19
Beauty and the Beast, 16-18
Beingessner, Laura, 10
Bell, Anthea, 12
Beneduce, Ann Keay, 24
Berenzy, Alix, 11
Bernoulli, Daniel, 15
Bettelheim, Bruno, 3, 11, 14, 17, 19, 24, 28
Birdseye, Tom, 25
Bound, 7
Breaking the Magic Spell: Radical Theories of Folk and Fairy Tales, 11, 22, 28, 125
Brett, Jan, 17
business card, 95
Buzzeo, Toni, xiv, 124

C

Caldecott, 9, 20, 23
Carreiro, Carolyn, 113, 124
Catrow, David, 8
cause and effect, 38, 41, 120
Cendrillon: A Caribbean Cinderella, 8
character, 49-55, 88-97, 116-117
character traits, 51
characters' physical descriptions, 90
Child, Lauren, 97, 124
Chiles for Benito/Chiles para Benito, 24
choral reading, 110-111, 122
Cinder Edna, 6
Cinderella, 2-10, 16, 46, 49, 57, 61, 79, 83, 95, 120, 124, 126
Cinderella Skeleton, 8
Cinderella, the Dog and Her Little Glass Slipper, 5
Cinderella: Three Hundred and Forty-Five Variants of Cinderella, Catskin, and Cap O' Rushes, abstracted and tabulated, 3
Cindy Ellen: A Wild Western Cinderella, 7
classic, 58
Classic Fairy Tales, The, 3, 14, 17, 19, 22, 24, 28, 125
climax, 34, 35, 36
Climo, Shirley, 3, 4
coat of arms, 51, 52
collaborate, xiii, 66, 113, 120
Collaborating to Meet Standards: Teacher/Librarian Partnerships for K-6, xiv, 124
COLLABORATION, xiii-xiv
compare and contrast, 66-68
Complete Book of Puppetry, The, 113, 125
comprehension, 31, 34, 37, 38, 41, 44, 46, 47, 49, 51, 54, 57, 73, 76, 83, 85, 86, 88, 93, 95, 98, 100, 101, 103, 105, 107, 109, 110, 111, 113, 114, 115, 116, 120
conclusion, 34, 35, 36, 37, 39
conflict, 38, 40, 41, 76, 77
Contemporary Drama Service, 115, 126
Contes des fées, i
context, 31, 49, 51, 54, 98
copyright, xvi, 37, 104, 111
Copyright Catechism: Practical Answers to Real Copyright Questions from Educators, xvi, 125
Copyright for Schools: A Practical Guide, xvi, 125
Copyright Responsibilities for Educators...Quick Pocket Guide, xvi, 125
Coretta Scott King Award, 9
Cox, Marian Roalfe, 3
Craft, K. V., 14
Craft, Mahlon F, 14
creativity, 83, 93, 111, 114, 115, 116
critical thinking, 37, 38, 41, 44, 47, 51, 57, 58, 66, 68, 69, 73, 74, 79, 82, 85, 86, 88, 93, 95, 98, 107, 109, 110, 111, 113, 114, 115, 116, 120
Cupid and Psyche, 16

D

Daly, Jude, 4
d'Aulnoy, Madame Catherine, xiii, 1
de Beaumont, Madame Le Prince, xiii, 16
de la Force, 10
de la Paz, Myra J., 4
de Paola, Tomie, 5
de Villeneuve, Madame Gabrielle Susanne Barbot de Gallon, 16
Defining the Fairy Tale, 1, 126
Delessert, Etienne, 20
Designing Rubrics for Reading and Language Arts, 65, 124
DeSpain, Pleasant, 25
dialogue, 49, 74, 75, 82, 85
Diaz, David, 10
dictionary, 1, 31, 32, 106
Disney, xv, 19
Do Tell! Storytelling for You and Your Students, 107, 125
Doney, Todd L.W., 15
Downes, Belinda, 20
Dragon Prince: A Chinese Beauty and the Beast Tale, The, 18
drama, 44, 113, 115
Dramatic Publishing, 115, 126
Duntze, Dorothée, 29

E

Egyptian Cinderella, The, 3
Ella Enchanted, 7, 49
Ella's Big Chance: A Jazz-Age Cinderella, 5
Ellis, John M., 21, 124
Elya, Susan Middleton, 97, 124
emotions, 54, 55
expression, 51, 54, 103, 105, 107, 110, 111

F

Fair, Brown & Trembling: An Irish Cinderella, 4
Fairy Tale Feasts: A Literary Cookbook for Young Readers and Eaters, 88, 125
Fairy Trails: A Story Told in English and Spanish, 97, 124
Fairytale as Art Form and Portrait of Man, The, 11, 125
Falling action, 34, 35, 36
Fee Fi Fo Fum: Puppets & Other Folktale Fun, 113, 124
Fiderer, Adele, 65, 124
Fletcher, Ralph, 86
fluency, 64, 103, 104-105, 107, 109, 110, 111, 113, 114, 115
40 Rubrics & Checklists to Assess Reading and Writing: Time-Saving Reproducible Forms and Great Strategies for Meaningful Assessment, 65, 124
fractured fairy tale, 85
"Fractured Fairy Tales & Fables with Jon Scieszka," 85
Fractured Fairy Tales: Puppet Plays & Patterns, 113, 125
Frey, Yvonne Amar, 113, 124
Fuller, Thomas E., 27

G

Galdone, Paul, 22
Gift of the Crocodile: A Cinderella Story, The, 9
Girl Who Spun Gold, The, 22
Glandon, Shan, 20, xiv, 124
Goode, Diane, 5
Gospel Cinderella, The, 10
"Grades 4-6: Due Process Freedoms, Yertle the Turtle Mock Trial," 127
Grimm, Jacob and Wilhelm, xiii, 2, 8, 10, 11, 12, 14, 19, 21, 23, 28, 29
Grimms' Fairy Tales: A History of Criticism on a Popular Classic, 14, 125
Griswold, Jerry, 17, 124
Groeber, Joan F., 65, 124
"Guide to Conducting Mock Trials," 120, 126
Gustafson, Chris, 112, 124

H

Haley, Gail E., 25
Hamilton, Virginia, 22
Hansel and Gretel, 28-29, 46, 49, 57, 86, 88, 110, 112, 120
Hard Facts of the Grimms' Fairy Tales, The, 28, 125
Harris, Jim, 12, 26
Harris, Marian, 12
Hastings, Waller, 1, 126
Hautzig, Deborah, 17
Heiner, Heidi Anne, 1, 3, 11, 14, 16, 17, 19, 21, 24, 28, 126
Heitman, Jane, 86, 124
"History of Beauty and the Beast," 16, 17, 126
"History of Cinderella," 3, 126
"History of Hansel and Gretel," 28, 126
"History of Jack and the Beanstalk," 24, 126
History of Mother Twaddle, and the Marvellous Atchievements of Her Son Jack, The, 24
"History of Rapunzel," 11, 126
"History of Rumpelstiltskin," 21, 126
"History of Sleeping Beauty," 14, 126
"History of Snow White and the Seven Dwarfs," 19, 126
Hoberman, Mary Ann, 105, 124
Hoffmann, Felix, 11
Hollenbeck, Kathleen M., 3, 124
Horosko, Marian, 15
"How to Become a Storyteller," 107, 126
How to Do "The Three Bears" with Two Hands: Performing with Puppets, 113, 125

"How to Make an Authentic Medieval Coat of Arms," 51, 126
Hughes, Shirley, 5
Humphrey, Albert, and the Flying Machine, 15

I

If the Shoe Fits: Voices from Cinderella, 10
inference, 44, 46, 51, 54, 57, 83, 88, 90, 93, 95, 97, 98, 100, 101, 116, 120
Information Literacy Standards for Student Learning, xi, 126
Information Power: Building Partnerships for Learning, xiv, 124
Integrating Technology: Effective Tools for Collaboration, xiv, 124
invitation, 83-84
IRA (International Reading Association), x
Irish Cinderlad, The, 4

J

Jack and the Bean Tree, 25
Jack and the Beanstalk, 23-27, 28, 97, 120
Jack and the Giant: A Story Full of Beans, 26
Jackson, Ellen B., 6
Jacob, Joseph, 24
Jaffe, Nina, 6
Janeczko, Paul, 86
Jarrell, Randall, 20
Jeffers, Susan, 29
Joe Cinders, 7
journalistic writing, 82

K

Kate and the Beanstalk, 26
Kathy Schrock's Guide for Educators, 65, 127
Keller, Emily Snowell, 15
Kennedy, John E., 115, 125
Kready, Laura F., 3, 125

L

Lasky, Kathryn, 15
Latshaw, George, 113, 125
Law Day—May 1, 127
Levine, Gail Carson, 7, 15
Listening, 105, 122-123
literacy communities, xi, 122
Little Gold Star: A Spanish American Cinderella Tale, 8
Ljungkvist, Laura, 20
Lohnes, Marilyn, 113, 125
Look Out, Jack! The Giant Is Back!, 25
Lorenz, Albert, 26
Lowell, Susan, 7
Lüthi, Max, 11, 28, 125

M

Mahlmann, Lewis, 113, 125

main action, 37-38, 76, 82, 120
Mak, Kam, 18
Make Your Own Puppets & Puppet Theaters, 113, 124
Martin, Rafe, 7
Martinez, Sergio, 8
Mayer, Marianna, 17
Mayer, Mercer, 17
McGlathery, James M., 14, 125
Mertz, Gayle, 127
Minkel, Walter, 113, 125
Mitchell, Kathy, 17
Mitchell, Marianne, 7
mock trial, 120-121
"Mock Trials," 120
Monster.com, 93, 127
Moser, Barry, 18
Mufaro's Beautiful Daughters: An African Tale, 9

N

Napoli, Donna Jo, 7
National Council of Teachers of English, xi, xii, 127
National Storytelling Network, 107, 126
NCTE, x, xv
Newbery Award, 7
newspapers, 82-83
Nichols, Beverly, 65, 125
19th Circuit Court of Lake & McHenry Counties, Illinois, 120
Nineteenth Judicial Circuit Court of Illinois, 126
Noël, Christopher, 22
North, Carol, 29

O

O'Malley, Kevin, 6
One Fairy Tale Too Many, 21, 124
One-Person Puppetry Streamlined and Simplified: With 38 Folktale Scripts, 113, 124
Opie, Iona and Peter Opie, 3, 14, 17, 19, 22, 24, 28, 110, 112, 125
Osborne, Mary Pope, 15, 26
Osborne, Will and Mary Pope Osborne, 15
Owl & Mouse Educational Software, 51, 126

P

Palazzo-Craig, Janet, 8
pattern recognition, 32, 47, 49, 66, 68, 83
Pentamerone, 19
Perceforest, 18
Perrault, Charles, xiii, 2, 5, 8, 9, 14, 15, 28
Persian Cinderella, The, 4
Pinkney, Brian, 8
Pioneer Drama Service, Inc., 115, 127
place, 57, 59, 74, 98, 100
Plays for Young Puppeteers: 25 Puppet Plays for Easy Performance, 113, 125
Playscripts, Inc., 115, 127
plot, 34-48, 68-79

poem, 86, 88
Poole, Josephine, 20
Potter, Giselle, 15, 26
predicting, 32, 44, 45, 51, 54, 57, 58, 68, 76, 79
presentation skills, 105, 109, 113, 115, 116
Princess Sonora and the Long Sleep, 15
Puppet Mania: The World's Most Incredible Puppet Making Book Ever, 113, 125
puppet theater, 85, 113-114, 122

R

Rabelais, Francois, 21
rap, 86
Rapunzel, 10-13, 46, 126
Rapunzel: A Fairy Tale, 12
Rapunzel: A Groovy Fairy Tale, 13
Ray, Jane, 29
Read Aloud, 103-106, 122
Read-Aloud Handbook, The, 103, 125
readers advisory, 47
Readers Theater, 85, 111-113, 122
READING, 31-65
recipe format, 88
Recipes.com, 88, 127
research skills, 58, 86, 88
résumé writing skills, 93-94
review, 61
Rhymes and Reasons: Using Poetry to Foster Literacy, 86, 124
rising action, 34, 35, 36, 68
Roberts, David, 13
Roberts, Lynn, 13
Rough-Face Girl, The, 7
RT, 111
Rubric, 63, 65, 101, 102, 106, 109, 115
Ruffins, Reynold, 9
Rumpelstiltskin, 21-23, 46, 47, 120
Rumpelstiltskin Problem, The, 23
Rumpelstiltskin's Daughter, 23

S

Sage, Alison, 22
Samuel French, Inc., 115, 127
San Souci, Robert D, 8
Sanderson, Ruth, 8
Santore, Charles, 21
Sathre, Vivian, 29
Scholastic Guides: Writing with Style, 66, 125
Schrock, Kathleen, 65, 127
Schroeder, Alan, 9
Schulz, J.C.F., 10
Scieszka, Jon, 85, 97, 125
script format, 85
Scripts for Schools, 85, 112, 126, 127
Scripts for Schools Choral Reading, 110
sequencing, 37, 68, 69
setting, 1, 34, 36, 48, 54-57, 59, 74, 75, 85, 98-100

Seven Dwarfs, The, 20
75 Language Arts Assessment Tools, 65, 125
Shepard, Aaron, 85, 112, 127
Shlichta, Joe, 25
Sierra, Judy, 9
Silin-Palmer, Pamela, 15
Simpson, Carol, xvi, 125
Sleeping Beauty, 14-16, 46, 126
Sleeping Beauty: The Ballet Story, 15
Sleeping Bobby, 15
Sleeping Bunny, 15
Sleeping Ugly, 16
Smoky Mountain Rose: An Appalachian Cinderella, 9
Sneed, Brad, 9
Snow White, 19-21, 46, 83, 88, 120, 126
Snow White and the Seven Dwarfs, 20
song, 86
Sootface: An Ojibwa Cinderella Story, 8
SPEAKING AND LISTENING, 103-123
Spellbinders, 107, 127
Spirin, Gennady, 22
STANDARDS FOR THE ENGLISH LANGUAGE ARTS, x-xi, 127
Stanley, Diane, 16
Stemple, Heidi E.Y., 125
Steptoe, John, 9
stereotyped character, 1, 49
Stinky Cheese Man & Other Fairly Stupid Tales, The, 85, 97, 125
story structure, 32, 34, 41, 44, 74, 76, 79, 82, 83, 85, 90, 97
Storytelling, 107-109
Storytelling Festival, 109
Strickland, Brad, 127
Strongheart Jack and the Beanstalk, 25
Study of Fairy Tales, A, 3, 125
Sullivan, Mary, 65, 125
Summer Reading Is Killing Me!, 97, 125
Super, Terri, 29
SurLaLune Fairy Tales, 3, 11, 14, 19, 21, 24, 28, 126

T

Tabart, Benjamin, 23
Tales from the Brothers Grimm and the Sisters Weird, 85, 125
Tales of the Fairys, 1
Talk Show, 116-119
Tam's Slipper: A Story from Vietnam, 8
Tang, Youshan, 4
Tatar, Maria, 28, 125
Tchaikovsky, 15
"Teacher Helpers: Assessment & Rubric Information," 65, 127
Teaching with Cinderella Stories from Around the World, 3, 124
Teaching Writing: Balancing Process and Product, 66, 125

theme, 48, 57-58, 60, 85, 100-101
Thomas, Joyce Carol, 10
Thompson, Stith, 2
time, 1, 48, 54, 56, 98
Tompkins, Gail E., 66, 125
Trelease, Jim, 103, 125
Trelease-on-Reading Web site, 103, 127
True Story of the 3 Little Pigs by A. Wolf, The, 85, 125
Tucker Pfeffercorn: An Old Story Retold, 22
Types of the Folktale, a Classification and Bibliography, The, 2, 3, 11, 14, 17, 19, 21, 24, 28, 124

U

unity, 32
Uses of Enchantment, 3, 11, 14, 17, 19, 24, 28, 124

V

Vande Velde, Vivian, 23, 85, 125
Vandergrift, Kay E., 19, 127
violence, 1-2, 14
vocabulary, 31
Vogt, Friederich, 14

W

Walker, Richard, 27
Wallace, Ian, 29
Way Meat Loves Salt, The, 6
Weissman, Annie, 107, 125
"What Is a Fairy Tale?," 1, 34, 126
When Dreams Came True: Classical Fairy Tales and Their Tradition, xiii, 11, 125
Whipple, Laura, 10
Who's Afraid of the Big Bad Book?, 97, 124
Willard, Nancy, 18

Wishbone, 27, 29
WRITING, 66-102
writing character descriptions, 93
writing comparisons, 66
writing contrasts, 68
writing nonfiction, 86
writing profiles, 90
writing story elements, 68-101

Y

Yep, Laurence, 18
Yolen, Jane, 16, 88, 125
You Read to Me, I'll Read to You, 105, 124
Young, Sue, 66, 125

Z

Zelinsky, Paul O., 13, 23
Zipes, Jack, xiii, 11, 22, 28, 125

	DATE DUE		

3 3743 00106270 8

PINGRY SCHOOL SHORT HILLS

3 3743 00106270 8   PRO 372.64 HE
Once upon a time : fairy tales

PINGRY SCHOOL SHORT HILLS